Look Beyond the Sleeping Dogs

Look Beyond the Sleeping Dogs

Portraits of a Vibrant Community in Park City's 'Ghost Town' Era

By Gary Kimball

Tramway Press

Published in the United States by
Tramway Press
Park City, Utah

ISBN: 979-8-9867036-0-2
Library of Congress Control Number: 2023901034

Book cover art by Harley Campos
Book cover and interior design by
Katie Mullaly, Surrogate Press®

Table of Contents

Part Two

Foreword

David Hampshire, April 2022

In the summer of 1986, when I was editing *Lodestar* (now *Park City Magazine*), I was contacted by a man who had written a series of essays recalling his years growing up in 1950s Park City. Many of them involved exploits in since-vanished Main Street watering holes. The essays were a bit rough, he said, but with a little polishing maybe we would consider publishing one or two.

The man was Gary Kimball, a descendant of the family that once operated the Kimball stagecoach and, later, Kimball's Garage, in the brick building that now houses retail stores on the northeast corner of Park and Heber Avenues.

Much has been written about Park City mining millionaires such as Thomas Kearns, David Keith and John Judge. But Gary didn't dwell on Park City's power brokers or the era of the great silver mines. He wanted to celebrate his friends and neighbors, people who were trying to eke out a living in an era when the mines were closing down and many folks were leaving town, sometimes taking their houses with them.

I was hooked. I loved his wit, his eye for detail, his profiles of the residents of the threadbare mining camp of his youth, and his anecdotes about teenage escapades, often involving awkward encounters with wary bartenders. More often than not, he was the foil of his own stories.

In the winter 1986-87 issue of the magazine we published his tribute to Maurine Foster, who ran a boardinghouse and small restaurant in the 1890s building known as the "concrete house" – which had survived the fire of 1898 and is still standing today – on the southeast corner of Park and Heber Avenues. I won't spoil the story other than to say that, in those bleak times, she resorted to other ways to pay the bills.

Gary's writing became a staple of the magazine. Accompanying most of his stories were whimsical illustrations by Don Weller, then the magazine's art director.

In 2006, Gary compiled about a dozen of these stories, plus a few that had not appeared in print, in a self-published book, "Of Moths and Miners and Other Tales of Old Park City." He also published three other books: "Death and Dying in Old Park City (2005), "Saloons of Old Park City" (2010) and "Life under China Bridge" (2013). In 2009, he was named Park City's official historian by the mayor and city council.

Later in life Gary shifted his attention to his earlier years, writing a series of personal essays focused mostly on his childhood in the late 1930s and 1940s. He planned to publish these as a companion volume to "Of Moths and Miners." I told him that I would be happy to work with him on that project.

Tragically, before these essays could be published, Gary died, in June 2018. His wife, Jane, died two years later. Since then "Of Moths and Miners" has gone out of print. After weighing the options, members of his family – his son and daughter, James and Janice Kimball, and his niece, Sarah Peters – decided to combine the new essays, "Growing Up in a Crumbling Town" (Part Two), in a book with a revised edition of "Of Moths and Miners" (Part One). Together with Gary's brother, Paul Kimball, they also sifted through family photographs and helped identify the people in them.

If you are tempted to skip over the Preface to Part One, don't. Gary's essay is the most insightful and eloquent of anything I have read about Park City in the 1950s. And in it you will also find a couple of paragraphs that were the inspiration for the title of this book.

I miss Gary. He was a gentle, humble man with a delightful, self-effacing sense of humor. I am honored to be able to play a part in bringing his stories to a new generation of readers.

PART ONE

Of Moths and Miners
and Other Tales of Old Park City

Dedication

In memory of those who gave a glimpse of their lives, and my wife Jane, whose encouragement and patience made this book possible.

Preface to Part One

Many of the articles in "Of Moths and Miners" (Part One) were originally published in *Park City (Lodestar) Magazine*. They are written, for the most part, about times in the 1940s, 1950s and early 1960s, a period in Park City's history that would best be described as its lowest ebb. The depressed mineral market, combined with labor problems, had closed most of the mines.

It was a time when the Utah State Highway Department realigned U.S. 40 and isolated Park City by another six miles.

It was a time when new highway maps had deleted Park City from their publications and many writers were referring to it as a ghost town.

It was a time when three out of five homes were vacant. Exploiters descended on the camp and bought many of the good homes for next to nothing, sometimes for only back taxes, then moved the houses to the Salt Lake Valley, turning a handsome profit. In the process they tore up the landscape, chopped down stately trees, and in many cases destroyed stone walls built with workmanship that could not be duplicated today. Those who protested this destruction were met with the reply, "There won't be nothing here in a few years except a memory."

It was a time when there was a large community of winos, derelicts and old-timers who were way out of proportion to the rest of the population. They did not have the means or the desire to seek the greener pastures that their neighbors were flocking to.

It was a time when store clerks and others in Salt Lake City and the surrounding communities would shun you upon learning that you were from Park City.

It was a time when the state was, on one hand, ready to write off the community as a ghost town while on the other hand condemning it as the greatest sin city between St. Louis and San Francisco.

It was a time that, when driving up Main Street on a Sunday afternoon, you might get the impression that the ghosts had already taken over. You might have to stop and wait for a sleeping dog to move, or to slow to a crawl to avoid hitting pigeons that would socialize by the hundreds on the street.

However, there was more life in Park City than sleeping dogs and congregating pigeons. If the Sunday drivers had gotten out of their cars and looked around, they would have found a vibrant, happy community. A proud, outgoing people with ready smiles and firm handshakes. A people who were proud of their past and hopeful for the future.

Park City was a real community. The joys and tragedies affected everyone. People cared for one another, worked together, played together and cried together. The citizens were tolerant and liberal. In every sense, the town was the classic American melting pot. Nearly every conceivable race, religion and political persuasion had come together. Ancient hatreds and mistrusts were forgotten in the Park City experience.

The common adversity of mines and mine management helped to bond the community together. Strikes and lockouts were a way of life. It was not that the miners hated the mine owners, but they had to show strength. During contract negotiations in the 1930s and '40s, one mine superintendent, George Kruger, was fond of saying, "We'll give you just what you're big enough to take and not one cent more." It did not pay to be weak in the owners' eyes.

The town was tolerant except with scabs. We were taught that scabs were the lowest of life forms and if they deserved to live at all, it was not in Park City.

Park City was never a hotbed of the far left. Probably the easiest way to sum up the attitude of the Park City miner is to repeat a conversation I overheard between a Butte, Montana, tramp miner and a local miner. The Butte miner was evidently well schooled in the traditional leftist arguments.

"Capitalism twists and uses the poor to exploit the working masses," his tirade began. "If we don't unite in brotherhood, they will continue with this wanton exploitation!"

The Park City miner, after some thought, replied, "Not only that, the tight bastards don't pay enough." Abstract ideals never carried as much weight as the pragmatic dollar to those who worked in Park City.

Park City entered the 1950s as it had in all other decades – with hope. But as time slowly passed, many businesses closed their doors. Even some people who still held jobs in the mines abandoned their homes in Park City and moved to Salt Lake, severing all ties with Park City except their paychecks.

There were some glimmers of false hope during this period, such as when the various independent mines consolidated to form the United Park City Mines Company in 1953. But with the depressed metal prices, the fanfare only amounted to a great community party. A one-night binge. The hangover lasted the rest of the decade.

Throughout its history, Park City had met and defeated every adversary it came upon: recessions, epidemics, avalanches, strikes, lockouts, mine cave-ins, mine explosions, fires. With stoic courage the camp survived.

Then in the 1960s an adversary crept into the camp that the natives were ill prepared to deal with. Prosperity! In 1962 the federal Area Redevelopment Agency loaned the United Park City Mines Company $1,232,000 from a fund designed to help depressed areas. With this money the company built the first phase of what is now Park City Mountain Resort. That, in turn, started the mindboggling skyward climb of Park City land values. Skiing was becoming the primary source of employment in the town.

Actually, it was a pseudo-prosperity. The jobs were seasonal and the wages were minimal. Many of the newcomers lacked the blue-collar work ethic that old Park City prided itself on. Many natives became alienated in their own hometown. People who had hung on in hard times were now glad to flee what Park City was becoming. At this writing less than five percent of the present population was here before skiing.

Park City was a gem; my stories reflect only a small facet of this precious stone. I realized that others who have lived the Park City experience will see it in a different light. But all will agree we are richer for the experience.

Of Moths and Miners

The Cozy as it looked in the 1970s. When you were going up the street, the sign read, "THE COZY – First Chance." On the reverse side, which you would see as you left Main Street, was, "THE COZY – Last Chance." A few people took the sign literally and called it the Last Chance Saloon ... and consumed their drinks as though the words would come true.
Photo courtesy of the Himes-Buck Digital Collection, Park City Museum.

The building wasn't much to look at. It was faced with blue tile that came into vogue in the 1930s. However, sometimes strange and wonderful things happened because of this blue tile. On warm nights in late summer, months by the thousands would swarm over the front of the building, attracted by the dancing red reflections of The Cozy's flickering neon sign. They made a mosaic of color and movement that was something to behold. But damn, if you hated flying, crawling things, it sure made it hard to go in or out.

From 1950 until the onset of the Park City skiing boom, The Cozy tavern marked the beginning of Park City's Main Street. In an earlier time there were business houses lower on the street, but by 1949 most were vacant lots. Ab Smith's house and coal scales survived, but that was about it below The Cozy.

The building was about 30 feet wide and 70 feet long. On the north side, running its length, was an 8-foot-wide annex that was used for storage. At one time, I understand, the annex housed a kitchen and The Cozy served the best steak dinners ever consumed in the camp, but that was way before my time.

During the mid-1960s Pete Solis set up a barbershop in this room every Thursday night, and I have to admit that it was the most congenial barbershop that I ever patronized. If you were lucky enough to get your haircut before 9 p.m., you wouldn't look half bad. After that hour you were taking your chances. But cold beer appeased everyone and the word was, "The only difference between a good haircut and a bad one is three days."

It was probably the only time in my life that I was consistently well groomed and, just my luck, it was a period when long hair was coming into vogue. But by then Thursday night had become a tradition, and I didn't like breaking traditions.

The bar stretched east to west for 20 feet along the north side of the main room. The bar stools were of chrome-plate tube construction and the vinyl-covered cushion seats were well worn.

The light oak back-bar, about 14 feet long and 10 feet high, was carved with scroll patterns. There was a large center mirror flanked by two smaller mirrors. Like the back-bars in the rest of the camp's saloons, it was cluttered with items for sale. The only unusual items I remember were fishing tackle, flies, and ammunition.

There were six booths – five along the south wall and one east of the bar on the north side – wired with an antiquated service-bell system. A black box mounted over the doorway to the annex would indicate a booth number and a bell would ring when a customer pressed a button at his booth. I don't remember this system ever being used with any success.

Hugh Steele, the owner, was a large-framed man. He stood about six feet two and was well equipped to handle any problems that might arise in his saloon.

As an adolescent, I would occasionally set pins in the War Memorial Building bowling alley. When Hugh bowled, we pinsetters would fight over the privilege of setting his alley. He was one of the few bowlers who ever bothered to tip pinsetters.

But there were some drawbacks. I've never seen anyone throw a bowling ball as hard as Hugh. The pins would go flying with such force that often several would land behind the protective barrier where the pinsetters huddled. The smarter pinsetters would usually seek protection in the next-lane bunker when Hugh was up.

Hugh, though, was a gentleman. He was soft-spoken and never used vulgarity. He usually wore a suit, always wore a dress hat, and favored a bow tie.

He worked the day shift in his tavern and was fond of saying, "What good is it being the boss if you can't set your own hours?"

Hugh enjoyed bird hunting and for years kept bird dogs. Every night at 9:30 in my neighborhood the quiet would be pierced by the sound of a dog whistle and Hugh calling his dogs. The Ten O'clock Whistle was never as precise. At times, though, his dogs would seek refuge nearby at The Cozy and could not hear their master's whistle over the drinkers' jovial babble. Hugh would phone the tavern and ask that the receiver be placed where the dogs could hear. I don't know what he told his dogs, but they sure got the hell out of there.

I never pushed my luck by trying to get served in The Cozy when I was underage. I had sold returnable soda-pop and beer bottles there since I was six or seven years old and bought all my .22 shells there. I didn't want to take the chance of being blackballed.

Empty returnable bottles were among my prime sources of revenue as an adolescent. My constant companion and great friend during this period was Ray Beckstead. Between the two of us we knew every family in our neighborhood that partied on weekends. In hindsight, I doubt that many of these fine people appreciated our beating on their front doors at eight on Sunday morning and asking for their empties, though we probably got a few of them off to church on time.

Emmett Sproul tended bar at The Cozy at night. He was easygoing and well liked. When he drank beer with his customers, his face and receding forehead would become beet red, but those were the only telltale signs.

When I first started to smoke, I used to buy cigarettes in The Cozy with the story that they were for my older brother. One night, after a year or so of this, I waltzed into the crowded tavern and asked, "Emmett, can I get a pack of Philip Morris for my brother?"

Emmett, with a straight face but dancing eyes, replied, "I don't know. Just a second and I'll ask him." He shouted down the bar, "Hey Gib! Is it okay if I sell a pack of smokes for you to your little brother?"

I didn't wait for the reply that was, no doubt, drowned out by hoots and laughter as I retreated out the door.

Emmett passed away in the late 1950s after a short illness. His place behind the bar was filled by Frank Nancarrow. Frank continued to work The Cozy until a short time after Hugh sold the establishment.

Generally, Frank was an okay bartender. Sometimes he would neglect the bar if he was in a tight game on one of the coin-operated pool tables. There were a few times when he got a little too drunk and forgot to lock up when he went home. Probably no one would have noticed if he had turned out the lights.

One group of independent miners was so loyal to The Cozy that they named their lease "The Cozy Dome" in honor of the tavern. United Park City Mines Company would, at times, lease underground workings to miners if the company itself could not turn a profit on the ground. Some lease miners made huge profits; others starved.

In time there were 19 miners working The Cozy Dome, one of the more profitable leases. "Working" might be the wrong word. Putting in time, at least a couple of hours a day, was more like it. The ore was so rich that they wisely held down their production. If they had shipped too much and their profits had become too huge, the mining company might have caught on and found a way to cancel their lease. Even so, their paychecks were double those of wage miners.

Of all the saloons in the camp, The Oak, at 415 Main, was probably the most liberal in buying drinks for its patrons. The house would pick up the tab on every third or fourth drink. The Cozy tradition was that each person at the bar would buy a drink for the bar, then the house would buy a round, then the process would repeat itself.

The system had its drawbacks. For example, everyone would end up drinking either bottle or can beer, even if he preferred draft. "I'll be damned if I'm going to drink ten-cent draft beer and buy everyone else two-bit bottle beer. Give me the same!" was the usual newcomer's response to the system.

There was one old patron who stayed away from this tradition and kept to himself. He was a railroad worker named Zip Nelson. After a few beers, Zip would start a conversation with imaginary friends. He would joke and laugh with them, rib them, discuss the events of the day, argue, and sometimes end up in a fight with one of them.

Actually, Zip was doing the very same thing as the rest of the house, but his friends were a lot cheaper to entertain and the injuries from his fights less severe. Why should he join in with the house when he had it all?

It was said that Zip at one time had supervised a section gang of Chinese workers and could speak the language. I know that at times it sounded like Chinese.

As far as I know, Hugh Steele always ran a clean operation – no gambling or liquor. He did pay off on the pinball machines and he had punchboards, but that was about it. I don't believe he had to worry about income like other saloon keepers when the economy went downhill. I do know that he had wealthy in-laws in Wyoming who, from time to time, would buy him a new car, and I suspect there were other remunerations.

Cozy owner Hugh Steele as he looked about 1930. *Photo courtesy of the Mel Fletcher Digital Collection, Park City Museum.*

In the early 1970s, Hugh's health, and his wife's, began to fail. Hugh was on crutches and knew his days were numbered. He honored a promise he had made years before to sell The Cozy to Fonce Martinez at a predetermined mining-camp price.

I knew The Cozy's days were numbered when Fonce's wife hung pink curtains in the windows. Frank Nancarrow was slow to adapt to the new owner's methods and was soon discharged. If Fonce could have spent more time with the business, perhaps The Cozy would have survived. But ill health made him an absentee landlord.

Eventually, all The Cozy had left was its reputation as the last of the old-time miners' saloons, and a house full of ski bums and tourists trying to find a miner.

The Cozy met its end in the last week of May 1979 when it was unceremoniously bulldozed to make way for yet another restaurant.

The Hidden Life of a Miner

A "motorman" guiding an electric locomotive in the Spiro Tunnel.
Photo courtesy of the Jordanelle Special Service District Collection, Park City Museum.

A short while back, on the sidewalk in front of my house, I overheard a conversation between a skier and his girlfriend. He was giving her the grand tour. In passing, he pointed out the Town Lift with the usual comments about convenience, etc. Then she asked him about the old Silver King Mine tramway tower that sits in my backyard.

"Oh that," he said. "That's the remains of an old ski lift that was abandoned a few years ago. Those towers were just too high. Can you imagine what would happen to a skier if he fell from that thing? I bet the liability insurance was outrageous ..."

I was amused at his ignorance. Even more, I was amazed. It's surprising how little many visitors and residents know about Park City's mining heritage.

Famous mines that once bore with pride such names as Queen Esther, Crescent, Three Kings and Silver King are now recalled only in the names of streets, condominiums, and chairlifts. Few cross-country skiers or summer bikers know the names of the tailings dumps that they pause on for a brief rest.

It's said that years ago Park City students could recite in a rhythmical meter the names of all 220 mines in the Park City district, with each refrain ending in, "But the Emma's gone." (The Emma was a famous mine in Alta.) Today's high school students are only vaguely aware of why they are known as the Park City Miners.

There's something hauntingly romantic about hard-rock mining, though I don't know a single miner who would admit to it. But once mining was in a man's blood, seldom would he seek other employment. There was a pride, a common bond that drew miners into a sense of camaraderie, a pride in knowing that few men would be able to do the job they did.

The layperson will never know the joking and horseplay that went on in the dry-room where miners would change into their diggers (work clothes), maybe gulping a last cup of coffee as they waited in line to pick up newly charged batteries for their headlamps.

The man-train soon was filled with the ingoing crew. A man-car was of simple construction: a two-inch plank about 10 inches wide and elevated about two feet above the floor of the car running the length of the car. The miners would straddle the board,

Miners loading a round of blasting powder. *Photo courtesy of the Jordanelle Special Service District Collection, Park City Museum.*

facing forward. As the train entered the portal, a cool breeze carrying an odor peculiar to mines would fan their faces. It's a musty odor, a combination of dry rot, spent blasting powder and God only knows what else.

Park City mines were a constant cool 48 degrees Fahrenheit, except for the New Park Mine, located east of Park City. Its temperature ranged to over 100 degrees.

The miners kept their heads down on the train so as not to be decapitated by low overhead timber. Most miners would not turn on their lamps until they arrived at the station, so the trip in was illuminated only by the headlight of the motor (electric engine) and the occasional sparks from the trolley pole as it skipped along the overhead power line.

Depending on where the miner worked, the trip to the job site could take more than half an hour. The Park City Mining District is a maze of tunnels, drifts, inclines, stopes, shafts and raises. There are more than 600 miles of underground workings in Park City, more mileage than in the New York City subway system. Now, of course, many of those workings have caved in or flooded.

Underground stations can be immense. The 600-foot-level station at the Ontario Mine could nearly hold the dome of the Utah State Capitol. Stations, electrified and well lighted, are the nerve centers of underground activities. Here there would be stores of timber, powder, tools, steel, and drill bits – all the supplies needed to keep a mine running smoothly.

Some stations even housed underground stables for horses – mostly geldings – and a few mules, until they were gradually phased out of the Park City mines during the late 1940s.

From the station, miners would descend in the cage (a mining elevator) to the various levels.

You don't know what darkness is until you experience the darkness of a mine. My only experience underground was in Climax, Colorado, because during the early 1960s the mines in Park City weren't hiring. It didn't take me long to discover that I did not like the dark or, for that matter, mining.

On my second day underground, the shifter dropped me off by myself to clean track in a drift. He was only gone for a short time when I noticed my lamp growing dimmer. As the pale, dull glow faded into nothingness, I found myself in a situation I hate – darkness! Total, complete dark, a nothingness, where minute sounds are amplified many times over. A falling pebble ... the sign of an impending cave-in? A drop of water ... the prelude to a flood? A distant echo ... maybe there's truth in all those ghost stories?

After a futile attempt to walk out, and three falls, I was completely turned around and didn't know which way was out. Besides, I had lost my lunch bucket.

After about four hours, the shifter (the man in charge of that section of the mine) came to my rescue. It seemed that none of the lamps on my shift had been recharged the night before and all had failed. Secretly, I made plans to quit mining as soon as I had a payday or two in my hip pocket.

Perhaps my quitting was hastened by the knowledge that the history of hard-rock mining is filled with death and tragedy. Ignorance and greed have killed or maimed thousands of young men. Now, through union and government action and the advance of technology, the industry has evolved to a point where most miners have a good chance of living long enough to collect Social Security. But in the early days of Park City, few miners lived to see their 50th birthdays.

Once it was common to store blasting powder and blasting caps in the same magazine. This practice resulted in the great explosion of 1902 that took the lives of 34 men at the Daly-West and Ontario mines (the two were connected by underground workings).

Lesser accidents were almost an everyday occurrence. Blasting accidents – "missed holes," in the parlance of the miners – happened when a miner picked or drilled into blasting powder that had not exploded in a previous blast. Overhead cave-ins, due to inadequate timbering or seams swollen from exposure to air, caused injury and death. The old saying, "Men are cheaper than timber" said it all.

In the shaft, poor equipment or improperly trained hoistmen were common. Falling tools, timber or rock also took their toll. Some men simply took missteps into shafts and were torn apart as they bounced off the walls; others drowned in the deep water in the bottom sump.

But the carnage of mine accidents couldn't compare with the deadly affliction of silicosis, known locally as "the con" (for miners' consumption), a disease caused by breathing the fine silica and quartz dust from drilling and blasting. In the early days, the cause of this disease was not understood. It was blamed on such factors at the dark, dank atmosphere of the mines or, for that matter, maybe the sins of the miners. With the advent of wet drilling and better ventilation, conditions slowly improved.

On the street, everyone who works in a mine is called a miner, but on the job it's quite another matter. A Park City miner was just that: he mined. He drilled holes with a jackleg or another type of drill; he loaded dynamite powder into the holes; he set the fuses and lit the charge at the appropriate time. He had to be able to judge the number of "shots" required to bring down an ore body, where to drill the holes, and how deep to drill for maximum effectiveness. He could recognize ore from waste rock and could judge the strength of the surrounding walls to determine if timbering were needed. Also, he needed enough skill in surveying to keep his working lined up.

Usually he had a helper called a mucker who "mucked" or cleaned up the blast site and helped the miner set up for the next round of drilling.

The timberman was the equivalent of a rough carpenter; he worked with heavy timber shoring up unstable ground. The art of installing a square-set of timber was fully appreciated only by the miners whose safety depended on the skill of the "artist".

The hoistman's job – running the cage (elevator) – was a heavy responsibility. He had to be alert and ready for the unexpected. A system of bell codes was used to signal instructions to the hoistman. The codes varied little from mine to mine. The standard signals were: three bells – bring men up; one bell – bring muck up;

A "hoistman" running the "cage" (elevator) at the top of the Thaynes Shaft.
Photo courtesy of the Jordanelle Special Service District Collection, Park City Museum.

one bell (if cage was already in motion) – stop. Each signal was followed by another signal to indicate the level that the sender was on. In an emergency, nine bells followed by the level signal would warn the hoistman so he could summon help or take other appropriate action.

The motorman ran the underground railroad that moved men, ore, timber and supplies. He had to get the trains in or out on a regular schedule. He had a helper known as a swamper whose main responsibility was to keep the motor pole or trolley boom always trailing behind the motor.

Of course, mines also had electricians, mechanics and blacksmiths, and one other important job should be mentioned: the job of the honey-dipper. The honey-dipper was in charge of underground sanitation. I'll let the reader's imagination fill in his duties.

Once the miner reached his work area, he and his mucker helper would set about mucking out the ore or waste overburden from the blasted face left by the preceding crew. Then they would set up the jackleg and the miner would begin drilling.

When it was time for lunch, they would make their way to the doghouse. The doghouse was a small wood structure that could seat six to eight men on benches along the walls. Often an electric heater and an electric light were installed. The doghouse could be counted on for warmth and dryness.

The Park City mines were usually wet. Depending on the location and the time of year, the moisture ranged from an occasional drip to something rivaling a cloudburst – where yellow wet-gear was a must.

During lunch there was time for small talk, sharing news and rumors, and some joking. At times the shifter would also drop in to have his lunch. The shifter was in charge of the crews in that section of the mine; the foreman was over the entire shift, which could number well over 150 men.

Depending on the skill of the miner, the afternoon could sail by. After he had completed his drilling, he would load his holes with powder and tap it in with a firm hand. The expression "tap it light" holds a certain meaning for many Park City natives.

After he had set his charge with blasting caps and had his fuse set, he and his mucker helper would sit back and wait. Each section of the mine adhered to a blasting schedule. If there was a crew farther down the stopes, the miners would wait until they came by and gave the word that everybody was out of that end. After lighting the fuse (electric blasting caps were usually reserved for extremely wet areas), the miner and mucker would make their way to the main tunnel and the waiting cage and begin the long trip to the surface.

A miner could settle into this routine but he could never drop his guard. Conditions were always changing. The ground could heave up, and was always pressing down, at times smashing huge timbers as though they were toothpicks. Huge pockets of ore or overburden could come crashing down without warning.

The very air could change without warning. Fear of gas – actually the lack of oxygen – haunted most miners. In the early days, before the advent of modern instruments, canaries were used to test the air in most of the mines. It's said that the Daly-West station was a regular aviary. When the air below was suspect, the men placed a canary in its cage and lowered it down the shaft. If the canary was still alive upon its return, then miners were lowered below.

Miners and canaries were not the sole occupants of the mines; mice and rats were also common, though their numbers dwindled after draft animals – and the grains that fed them – were discontinued.

For the most part, miners considered rats as good-luck omens and seldom did them harm. After all, rats did clean up food scraps that would otherwise rot and foul the air. And many miners considered them to be an early warning system of an impending cave-in. Rats would sense the shifting ground and flee, alerting miners to impending danger.

The strangest animals, to my knowledge, ever to take up residence underground were beavers! Some years ago a colony of three made their way through a drain tunnel to the bottom of the Ontario Number Six Shaft, a location nearly three miles from the portal. There the beavers set up housekeeping and nearly drove a Kamas miner crazy.

This miner prided himself on his trapping skills that, he said, would rival Jim Bridger's. But it was only after several weeks and many sleepless nights that he finally rid the mine of these intruders and redeemed his reputation. After that he boasted of being the world's only underground trapper.

Mining was not all work. The miners would take delight in testing the mettle of all new employees. The temperament of each "dude" or "greenhorn" was soon found out. After all, the very lives of everyone could, in times to come, depend on the new employee's skill and judgment. An informal initiation was a way to see if he was made of the right stuff. Besides, it was fun.

One favorite trick was to coat the sweatband of the new man's hardhat with a broken stick of powder. This would cause an almost instantaneous "powder headache." Few people outside of hard-rock mining are familiar with this affliction. Some substance in nitroglycerin causes a most peculiar and painful headache.

When a new employee developed this powder headache, some old callous miner would almost always suggest that the dude place a "wee bit" of powder under his tongue for an instant cure. Then he would sit back and watch as the poor man developed an even more excruciating headache. When the sufferer left the mine, the headache would always vanish with the first blast of fresh air.

Another sport reserved for belligerent young miners, especially on the eve of their weddings, was to coat them with cable grease. This grease seemed impervious to the strongest soap, and only patient scrubbing could save a man from a most embarrassing situation.

Most young miners were also primed with lore about ghosts and haunted mines, and in time some became true believers.

Occasionally, though, the tables were turned. While working at the Alliance Mine, a miner named Skully died of an apparent heart attack. He had been working alone in a stope accessed by an incline of about 60 degrees, 200 feet above the main tunnel.

The shifter had a hard time recruiting a miner to take Skully's place. No one wanted to work where a death had recently occurred. After much wrangling and browbeating, Pat Pagan, known locally as "Patty the Pig" because of his renowned feats at the dinner table, spoke up.

"I'll do it! I'm no coward like some that I could name. By God, I'll do it."

Patty was an Irish miner of considerable skill. About an hour into his hand-picking, Patty had settled into a routine. But unknown to him, young Con O'Neil, whose father was the famed superintendent at the Silver King Mine, had sneaked through the workings and came into the stope from a higher frontal direction. Holding his lamp low and shaded by his hand, he called, "Why have you taken my place, Patty? This is my place ... Why are you here? This is my job."

The shadowy figure slowly advanced, calling to Patty, continuing to ask why he was in his workplace.

The shaken Patty later recalled, "I backed to the incline as fast as a man could run, and I flew down the ladder, only hitting my bum three times on the rungs as I came down. I landed on my hands and knees but, looking up, I could see him still following me, calling my name and asking why I had taken his job.

"Down the portal I ran, hoping to find safety with my friends. I ran 'til I could run no more, so I stopped and said, 'God damn it Skully, if you want me, come and get me. I'm ready for you.'

"The whole crew greeted me with howls of laughter. But you know, if I live to be a hundred, I'll never enter that stope again."

The time is approaching when Park City's mines and miners will be only a footnote in a history book. But I do hope that sometime, when you are on an outing and you find yourself on some forgotten mine tailing dump, you will take a few moments and think of those who first brought Park City its fame.

The Park Tavern

Mike Safianides and a member of his staff outside the Park Tavern in 1946.
Photo courtesy of the Kendall Webb Collection, Park City Museum.

I can still remember my first experience with the Park Tavern, though it was back in 1951.

As a freshman in high school I seldom missed a change of movies at the Egyptian Theatre. But the Egyptian did not sell popcorn, candy or soft drinks at that time and Chick Lloyd, the owner, frowned on patrons who tried to sneak them onto the premises. Not that that prevented most students from taking some treat with them. The challenge of putting one over on Chick Lloyd was nearly as enjoyable as the treat itself.

One night we were late for the show and did not stop on the way for candy or a soft drink. However, on reaching the Egyptian,

Bob, my companion, continued up the street. He told me he was going to the Park Tavern to buy a bottle of Coke and tried to talk me into doing the same.

Now, I had only 50 cents and the price of admission was 45 cents, so I waited on the sidewalk for Bob, growing a little angry with the passing minutes. We were missing the beginning of the movie.

Finally a bewildered Bob came out of the tavern carrying a brown paper sack and motioned me to follow him around the side of the building down to Swede Alley. There under a street light he showed me a quart of Coors beer. He told me that all he did was ask for a Coke and the old Greek behind the counter cursed him like hell, returned with the beer, rang up the 50-cent sale, and would only shrug at Bob's protest.

By then Bob did not have enough money for the movie, and he was convinced that drinking the beer would be more fun anyway. So he did his best to convince me that it was my moral obligation to forgo the movie, march into that tavern and demand a bottle of Coke ... or whatever.

Well, I caved in. I knew I could not enjoy the movie if one of my best buddies was out having a great time without me. Besides, the show by now was half over. So I mustered up all my courage and marched up to the swinging door, peeked through the window, said a silent prayer, swallowed hard and went in. God I was scared.

The place was empty except for old Mike Safianides and he was asleep, head cradled in his arms at the other end of the bar. I cleared my throat several times hoping to wake him, all to no avail. In sheer desperation I slapped my four-bit piece down on the bar.

He stirred, his eyes studying me. Slowly he got up, muttering, and slowly shuffled toward me.

I didn't have the courage to look at the old man who at this moment seemed to hold my fate in his hands. Instead I studied my surroundings until my eyes fell on a four-point deer-head trophy mounted behind the bar. Later I would learn that some of the steady customers referred to this trophy as Ralph.

Ralph was, under other circumstances, well worth studying. He was a perpetual ornament, with garlands and tinsel draped on him in a most becoming fashion. To set it all off there was a cigar stub in his mouth.

Mike Safianides spoke poor English, but he sure could cuss, as I was about to learn.

"Jesus o' Christ, what you want? Son o' bitch, you boys get me in trouble all the time ... Son o' bitch comes in here, wants beer. How many? One? Quart? Church key? Okay, okay, son o' bitch. Last time. No more. Jesus o' Christ, son o' bitch, Chuck (City Marshal Chuck Thomas) will have me in jail."

The interior of the Park Tavern as it looked in 1949.
That's owner Mike Safianides facing the camera in front of the window.
Photo courtesy of the Kendall Webb Collection, Park City Museum.

Shrugging his shoulders, he sacked up a quart of Coors and dropped a bottle opener into the sack. I don't think I said a thing. Just nodded in agreement. As he rang up the sale on a turn-of-the-century cash register, he kept up a steady string of oaths, some in English, most in tongues that were foreign to my ears.

When Mike handed me the sack and I left the tavern, I felt a relief that nearly sent me dancing down the alley to my waiting friend.

As you can guess, this date marked a decline in my movie-going days.

Later, when our group became accepted as regulars at the Park Tavern, we would always sit in the booth nearest the jukebox, and much to Mike's consternation we would order our Coors by the quart at 50 cents a bottle instead of the standard 11-ounce 25-cent bottle.

Park City on the whole was pro-union, liberal and staunchly Democratic, while the Coors family has always been known as anti-union and as oppressive as conservative Republicans can be. Yet there was a great loyalty in Park City to Coors beer.

One reason that Coors was popular was because of Alex S. Mark, known to one and all as Tuffy, the senior partner in M&M Distributing Company, the Coors beer distributor. Dark hair, loud and friendly, a perpetual chewed cigar in his mouth, Tuffy was a stout, powerful man, as his nickname implies. He and his crew would reach town on Thursday afternoon and would stretch their deliveries until late that night.

We used to joke about Larry Bye, a town rounder who would show up at each tavern just before Tuffy made his delivery. Larry knew that Tuffy would always buy one or two rounds for the house and it was to his credit that he never missed one.

At times you would see drinks bought *for* the house at the Park Tavern, but never drinks bought *by* the house. Mike Safianides did not believe in the old Park City custom. The only time I ever saw Mike buy drinks was when he was attempting to prevent a fight between arguing customers, and then just for the warring factions.

He had a reputation for being close-fisted, but there was method to his madness. One night after he had refused to loan a good customer five dollars and the irate miner left in a huff, I asked Mike to explain why. After all, the man had a good reputation for paying his debts, if somewhat slowly.

Mike, in his broken English, explained: "Son o' bitch, if I give him money he buy one, maybe two beers here, then go down the street and spend it there. Jesus o' Christ, son o' bitch no come back here maybe one, two weeks. He no come back 'til he got enough money to pay me. 'Til then he gives his business to son o' bitch down the street.

"Ha, ha, now he borrows some money down the street, son o' bitch won't go back there 'til he can pay money back. Ha, ha, now maybe he come here."

Mike Safianides never seemed to change. The old Greek appeared the same the first time I saw him as the last. Short – about five foot five – rounded shoulders, no neck, and plump. He was a Neanderthal. Lynn Gordon used to claim that Mike was living proof of evolution.

"Hell, look at that receding forehead, those dark beady eyes set close together, that broad nose, thin lips, that wide mouth, and those teeth. Hell, if they weren't so worn down he'd look ferocious. Yap, if Darwin was alive today, he'd use Mike to prove his theory."

I spent many of the slower evenings visiting with Lynn Gordon. Lynn ran the blackjack table and his mere appearance could lull the most prudent gambler into a sense of self-confidence. He was crippled with arthritis; his once tall frame was bent and twisted, and he could only walk with the aid of crutches. Skin stretched over bone gave him a near skeletal appearance until you looked into his eyes. They danced.

Lynn's soft voice was authoritative. He had vast knowledge on many topics that only occasionally revealed he was self-taught.

His fingers were crooked and his fingernails were exceedingly long. Nails and fingers were stained bronze from cigarette smoke. To watch him clumsily shuffle a deck of cards would make a person think that he was in the wrong occupation.

But Lynn had talents. He could talk for hours about the strategy and the odds of the game. He would demonstrate how, by sound alone, you could tell if cards were being dealt from the bottom of the deck. He would advise me where to sit at a table to best observe the dealer depending on whether he was left- or right-handed. But as far as I know he never used this knowledge to cheat any of his customers.

Lynn's interests were diverse; he loved to discuss philosophy and politics. He was one of the few people in a Park City tavern who would openly boast of being a Republican. Though he was a Mormon by birth, his religious views tended to be agnostic. With eyes bright with wine, he would often recite verses from the Rubaiyat of Omar Khayyam.

And deep in wine he was. Beer he rejected as too filling. "Hell, as slow as I travel on these crutches, by the time I get back from the john I'd have to turn around and go again." Hard liquor he rejected because it dulled his senses, and as a dealer he had to be sharp.

A few years later, after the big raid, Lynn became Park City's sole bootlegger. Then he rejected consuming hard liquor with, "One never mixes business with pleasure."

The big raid took place on the night of April 16, 1955. The state of Utah, sensing that the old mining camp was in its death throes and too weak to resist, decided to put an end to something that, though American, it found repugnant.

Sixty troopers, a blend of state law officers and zealot farmers from Summit County, raided all the suspect establishments simultaneously. It was rumored that the reason the troopers knew their way around so well was that many were old customers.

The newspaper reported that the plans of this raid were a well-kept secret, and that Summit County Sheriff George Fisher was not even notified until five minutes before it started. But I don't believe that was the case.

The night of the raid about five of my classmates and I stopped in the Park Tavern. No sooner had we sat down than the night officer, Bob Evans, came in. I still remember him saying, "Not tonight boys. Out!"

It wasn't what he said or even how he said it. We had been hassled before and usually had alternative plans for the evening. But something made us heed his advice.

I'm glad we did. In my own mind I'm sure that he had advance warning of the raid and went out a limb to save some kids much embarrassment.

The state locked the doors of four taverns, one hotel and one house of ill-repute that night. Bessie's, the most famous of the camp's sporting houses, was found empty. Common knowledge had it she was tipped in advance.

The Park Tavern was one of the four that was closed that night. Mike and Lynn were taken into custody, although the state knew there was little chance of getting a conviction from a jury: a deaf old Greek and a dealer who was crippled! Besides, they couldn't find any booze, except about a third of a pint that Mike maintained was his, and not for sale. I was told the troopers literally tore the place apart.

Years later I learned where the stash was hidden. Mike had a cigarette case on the counter behind the bar. The front that held the cigarettes was built in a terraced manner. It was hinged and would lift up to reveal a sizable hiding place. I was told that the night of the raid there were 33 pints hidden there.

After the big raid, when liquor was no longer sold over the bar in Park City, Lynn went into business for himself. He would buy Seagram's Seven blended whiskey for $2.43 a pint from the state liquor store and resell it for five dollars a pint after the state store was closed. He had a good late-night and holiday business.

Lynn's only problem was that he was unable to get to the liquor store and would use most anyone to tram for him. Not long after I was discharged from the Navy I received a phone call at home from Lynn one afternoon. It was somewhat clandestine because of the old central telephone system and the tendency the operators had to eavesdrop.

The building as it looked in the late 1970s as The Red Banjo.
The Bull Durham sign had just been restored by local craftsman Norm Hall.
This view is now blocked by an adjacent structure.
Photo courtesy of the Mary Lou Toly Digital Collection, Park City Museum.

"Gary, how about doing me a favor."

"Sure, Lynn, what do you want?"

"Would you go to the lumber yard for me and pick up some nails?"

"Lumber yard and get some nails?"

"Ya, Utah Coal and Lumber and get me a dozen seven-penny nails, the type of Seven that I always use. Get a dozen and I will reimburse you when you deliver."

If I could figure out his code I'm sure most of our telephone operators could too, but it was a fun game. So I went to the Utah Coal and Lumber Company, which had the Park City franchise for the state liquor store, and bought a dozen pints of Seagram's Seven for Lynn. For the next several years I'd tram for Lynn whenever his regular connections fell through.

Mike didn't think much of Lynn conducting his business from the Park Tavern but tolerated it because it brought him some side trade. Lynn more than once remarked, "The old Greek would run me out of here like he does with the other winos if I wasn't good for business. In a way we feed off each other."

In a way Lynn's comments could apply to all of Park City of that period. With the mines closed, the town fed on itself. A sort of cannibalism without malice, its only aim – to survive. Full houses were then few and far between, confined usually to weekends and holidays. But few ever thought that Park City would really die. There had been hard times before and the old camp had survived. It would again.

Times change and people age. Lynn's health deteriorated to the point that he had to seek care in the old Miners Hospital and was never again able to take his place at the Park Tavern. Even the old Greek, who never seemed to change, did grow older and slower. His relatives in Salt Lake convinced him to sell the business. The door was closed for the last time on a summer night in 1962.

I still remember the last time I saw him. I stopped in the building that only a few days before had housed the Park Tavern. A friend of mine was the proud new owner and was busy ripping out booths and partitions and stripping paint from the old back bar. The walls were being covered with barn lumber. It was a complete new look.

Mike, after greeting everyone, slowly walked around the once-familiar building. No one else noticed as he shuffled out the door, quietly muttering, "Jesus o' Christ, a good place, now a barn. Son o' bitch wanted a barn, he could have had my old shack. What's a man to do? Son o' bitch crazy."

I'm not sure, but I think there were tears in his eyes. To my knowledge Mike never returned.

Editor's note:

In the original edition of "Of Moths and Miners," the author settled on "Sofinades" for the name of the old Greek who ran the Park Tavern. He may have used that spelling because it appeared in The Park Record's *story describing the great raid in April 1955. However, he had plenty of other choices. Between 1934 and 1955, the name of the Park Tavern proprietor is spelled at least a dozen different ways in the pages of* The Park Record. *For this edition, we settled on "Safianides" because it is spelled that way in ads for the Park Tavern – that Mike presumably approved – which ran in* The Park Record *several times in 1934.*

On the other hand, the paper is consistent in one respect: His first name is always spelled M-i-k-e.

Incidentally, there is also some disagreement as to Safianides's country of origin. The author says it was Greece. However, in a July 1950 story, The Park Record *told its readers that he was taking a vacation in his native country of Turkey.*

Big Wayne

Big Wayne mugs for the camera in this 1979 Park Record photograph. In his left hand he holds the fuse to what is purported to be a stick of dynamite attached to the top of his hat. At this time he was responsible for rattling Park City residents awake on the Fourth of July and Labor Day with the traditional sunrise dynamite salute on Masonic Hill. *Photo courtesy of The Park Record.*

I don't know why it is, but what you have is never as good as what you want.

Back in the 1950s, Park City girls were as pretty as any girls in the state. The problem was, they were here.

Now if you wanted pretty, Heber was the place to be. That was drilled into us for as long as I can remember. Older boys who had just returned from Heber would, when questioned by their buddies, always give a knowing high sign, then would go off whispering together. We grew up thinking that Heber must have been some sort of paradise.

When he was in the seventh grade, Big Wayne sluffed school one morning. About two that afternoon, he returned from Heber with stories of glorious conquests. Six different girls! Each for a couple of hours. The glory, the power, the beauty. Oh, the envy we had for him. Big Wayne was held in high esteem.

His tales, if put into a mathematical time frame, would have compressed 12 hours into a five-hour period, and that might have conflicted with the math concepts that Coach Reeves was trying to drill into us. But if Big Wayne proclaimed this, it must be so.

Big Wayne was different, and was often the center of attention. He once showed up in class with a great horned owl. He was on a first-name basis with every unsavory character in the camp. When the carnival was in town, he would be the one who got the job.

One Labor Day even the most skeptical of our group became convinced of Wayne's special qualities. That year the big bash was held at the City Grove (in what the members of the Rotary Club now call their park). With all its usual activities – races, games, food, drink and music – it was a fine day. At one point, Big Wayne excused himself and made his way across the tiny willow-clogged creek to relieve himself.

He soon returned, claiming he had done a world first, and beckoned us to follow him through the rough terrain. When we arrived, an astonishing sight awaited us. There lay a crop so fresh that the blue flies were only then finding the stench, and behold – it was bright green!

None of us had ever seen or heard of such a thing. It must have been a world first. And only one as grand as Big Wayne would have shared such a thing with the likes of us.

Yes, Big Wayne was different, and if he said something, it must be so. Coach Reeves' math class was not only boring, it was in error.

Wayne knew everyone and had many friends; everyone liked him. But he was a loner. At times he would chum with one group or another, but more often than not he was alone. He'd disappear from school sometimes for days on end and usually come back with tales of great adventure.

Once he returned in sorry shape. He had a black eye that was swollen nearly closed, a swollen nose, and other wounds that were scabbing over.

Big Wayne's story was scary, but good. He had skipped school to visit one of his girlfriends in Salt Lake City when he was jumped by members of the Spud Gang. "Dropped three of them, including Spud, before they got me from behind."

Studying our wide eyes, he warned, "Watch out for the Spud Gang!"

I had never heard of the Spud Gang before, and I've never heard of them since. But for years I was cautious. In fact, I still don't feel comfortable with people from Salt Lake until I know for sure that they don't have any connections with the Spud Gang.

At times Wayne would allow me to hang out with him. These occasions usually fell on cold, stormy days. Those days when only fools would venture out.

Once, in the absence of Marshal Chuck Thomas, we hung out at the police station in the old City Hall on Main Street. Big Wayne had a new pet with him, a young magpie that he named Bishop, and he had taught it to smoke.

There we sat, feet perched up on the marshal's desk, smoking Wayne's Lucky Strike cigarettes. Wayne occasionally would stick his lighted smoke into the bird's beak, and I swear that magpie seemed to enjoy it. Wayne said the bird know how to talk but had a sore throat from smoking too much. He said he was trying to get the bird to cut down.

It didn't matter to me if the bird didn't speak. It couldn't get better than this. The cast-iron radiator hissed out grand warmth, and there was the thrill of using the john in the unlocked cell. It seemed like some sort of forbidden fruit – delicious.

Wayne told me about the time that Juvenile Judge Clark had him thrown into the dungeon in the basement of City Hall for several days, and how he had to keep awake at night to fight off the rats. He wouldn't tell me about his crime, except that it was too hideous to speak of. He showed me the huge pocketknife he had in case he ran into the Spud Gang again. We talked about the girls of Heber, and he told me to look up the McCarty twins, the hottest numbers in the valley. I thought that I'd heard them mentioned before and made a mental note to remember the name.

Unfortunately, I've always been bad at remembering names. After I got my driver's license and started making solo trips to Heber, I looked for the twins, all to no avail. Of course, when asked about Heber by my friends, I told them about the MacArthur twins and, much to my chagrin, invented a legend that grew rapidly. Soon my friends wanted to compare notes with me about these sirens. So seductive was their reputation that I actually started looking for them myself.

A few years after our winter afternoon in the police station, I had a double date with Big Wayne. Wayne's date was a Park City girl and mine was a girl from Heber.

Wayne's car was in bad shape. The battery was shot. It was okay in Park City, where it could always be parked on a hill. But on the flat land of Heber or Salt Lake it gave one the unneeded exercise of pushing, and more pushing, to get it started by compression. It didn't matter. It was the price of good company.

We took the girls to Liberty Park in Salt Lake City and enjoyed all the rides and cotton candy, and floated around on the small lake in pedal-powered boats. The girls giggled with glee at the final exhausting push as the car sputtered into motion for our trip home.

Big Wayne turned out to be a perfect gentleman. Of course, I reasoned, he was with a Park City girl and knew he couldn't get too fresh. I worried that he would think less of me because my date was from Heber but I followed his lead and acted like a gentleman.

Later, when asked about our dates by envious friends, Wayne gave me a nudge and a high sign, saying, "We don't talk about our lady friends."

We walked off together, whispering.

Wayne Rex Putman, the fourth of five children, was nearly eight years old when he enrolled in the first grade. By the sixth grade he

Shown here as a mature high school freshman in 1952, Wayne was at least a year older than most of his classmates. *Photo courtesy of Park City High School 1952 yearbook.*

had stopped growing in height at about five feet nine inches but continued to fill out.

Wayne dropped out of high school our sophomore year at the height of the Korean conflict and enlisted in the Air Force. Later, he spent many years working the mines in Park City. After their closure, he became an equipment operator for the Park City Municipal Corporation.

Wayne never fully gave up the limelight. He was a big hit as a rodeo clown and, for many years at Christmas, he delighted children as Santa Claus. Known to many as Put-Put, he was a local champion arm-wrestler. And every Fourth of July and Labor Day he set off the traditional dynamite sunrise salute.

Stricken by a massive coronary, Wayne died in December 1982 at age 46.

Bars for the Bartender

Erected about 1900, this building was occupied by Davich's Bar and Grill for many years. This photo of the building as the Handle Bar was taken about 1963. At this writing (2022) it is the home of the Firewood restaurant.
Photo courtesy of the PCHS Collection, Park City Museum.

I remember the first time I was served at Davich's Bar and Grill. I was a sophomore in high school and, after a school basketball game one Friday night in 1952, I wandered uptown instead of going to the dance that followed the game.

In Pop Jenks' Café I was joined by Ed, an upperclassman and a member of the basketball team. He suggested we go up the street and have a beer.

I thought he meant the Park Tavern, where I was already a regular. But when he walked past that establishment and on toward

The Grill, I was petrified. Ed, I guess, did not want to run into any of his peers who frequented the Park Tavern.

I tried to convince him that I would not be admitted to The Grill. But he contended that, if I behaved and acted my age, I would not have any trouble. You could lay money on the fact that, as we swung through the swinging doors, I was the most dignified 16-year-old you would ever behold.

Joe Davich and his brother-in-law, Benny Bircumshaw, both were behind the bar, but it was a quiet night. I don't recall anyone else being there except Charley Thompson sitting alone at the end of the bar.

Charley handled the blackjack table that was located directly opposite the bar along the north wall. He was a quiet, soft-spoken man who could blend into the crowd. This ability saved him much hassle the night of the big raid. He simply stepped around his blackjack table and was kicked out of the tavern by the deputies along with the paying customers.

Joe and Benny were both in a jovial mood, and there was a lot of good-natured kidding. I soon began to relax. That was an error on my part. I knocked over my third glass of draft beer. Hoots and laughter followed, and I wished I could have crawled into the woodwork.

After Joe had wiped up the spill, he drew a short beer with the admonition, "Three beers and Kimball's getting drunk. From now on it's short beers for him!"

From then on, when I was at Joe's, I would be served only three regular drafts of Coors, and from then on only short beers. He never said a thing. There was a subtle wink, but he never cracked a smile.

It could have been worse. One of our group, Dean Hansen, could not get served at all. Dean's father, Russ, had left specific instructions with Joe not to serve his son.

The first time Dean was with us at The Grill, Joe accepted our order for beers all around but served one short, substituting a bottle of Coke for Dean and proclaiming loudly, "No beer for Boomer!"

Poor Dean. Not only was he never served a beer at Joe's, but he also gained the instant nickname "Boomer." It stuck with him for the rest of his life.

Davich's Bar and Grill was located at 304 Main Street, now (in 2022) the home of the Firewood restaurant. It was always a favorite of Park City's locals. It was said that, during Prohibition, John Davich, Joe's father, had secret rooms and tunnels in the basement to hide bootlegging activities. But years later, when the basement was remodeled, nothing was found. Perhaps the modern-era contractors, with their shortcut methods, missed finding the historic curios of the past. Maybe they destroyed them without knowing what they found.

The Grill was a large tavern by any standard. Most of the action was in the taproom, or barroom, which occupied the northwest section of the building. The ancient mahogany-stained back-bar was about 20 feet long and ran parallel to the center wall that partitioned the front of the building. In keeping with Park City tradition, it was cluttered with glasses and items for sale. The southwest section housed a billiard room. The rest of the building opened into a huge dance hall; there were booths all along the north and south walls.

Joe Davich quit mortician school to take over the management of The Grill when his father died in 1953. Joe was outgoing, cheerful, and a fast wit.

"Hell, I'm the only barkeeper in the camp who has been schooled in the art of pickling," he would joke, "and I can pickle my customers with a finesse the other barkeeps can only envy."

Joe was considered an up-and-coming businessman, and many thought he was destined for a great future. On June 4, 1953, he was appointed to fill a vacancy on Park City's City Council when incumbent Councilman George Keating resigned and left town for a short while.

Joe was a true Park City booster. He worked hard in civic clubs and government to give life and spirit to the dying camp. With the mines closed and many businesses boarded up, many citizens sought greener pastures. Hardly a week would go by without one or two families leaving. But Joe had faith in the camp and the wealth of the mountains and knew that, in time, the economy would turn around. All you had to do was believe and be patient. Everyone wanted to believe him; some actually did.

Unfortunately, Joe's career was cut short. He was caught in the big raid of April 16, 1955.

Raids in Park City were a common occurrence. They were often conducted by the county sheriff, George Fisher. Once or twice the federal government was involved, but more often the government was represented by the Park City marshal.

To the city, the fines they generated were a desperately needed form of revenue. Park City was broke. The mayor and councilmen, unlike those of today, worked for free. Perhaps they resorted to these extraordinary means in order to keep the roads plowed, the graves dug, the water running, and to meet the payroll. To this day I cannot find fault.

In April of 1955, when rural Summit County and the state of Utah sensed the death throes of the old mining camp, it boosted their moral indignation to a new high. Members of the dominant Utah culture had never fully accepted the idea of a gentile island in their sea. They considered Park City a vile hell-hole that corrupted their sons. They would put an end to this degradation once and for all! Led by Summit County Attorney Morgan W. Lewis, 60 state and county deputies raided four taverns, one hotel and one house of ill-repute.

Park City Mayor Tom Costas was enraged. He deputized more than 100 Park City men and removed the locks placed on the establishments by the county.

It didn't matter. The game was up. Governor J. Bracken Lee and the courts sided with the county and Park City's slide into oblivion was assured. Or so they thought.

Joe Davich was the only operator caught in the raid to serve any time in prison. In all likelihood the state authorities came down on Joe because he was a city councilman.

The Grill would never reopen under that name, or Davich's management. After he served his sentence, he returned to school, then worked as a mortician in Salt Lake City until his death.

Strong Coffee, Cheap Sex

Maurine Foster illustration by Don Weller.

Maurine Foster was huge. She was really, really fat. Today they call it obese.

I've always tried to use that term sparingly, but with Maurine it was fitting. Her black '51 Ford tilted so far to the left that the tires on that side looked flat. Both the front and rear springs on the driver's side were broken.

Maurine was married to a mechanic who worked at the Silver King mill. He was known as Slim and stood six foot six. Because of his height and Maurine's weight, he was subjected to a lot of good-natured kidding in the mine's dry (locker) room. He would take it all in stride and reply with a grin, "It's like swimming upstream, but more fun."

Maurine ran a boardinghouse and small restaurant in a building which many old-timers referred to as the "concrete house." A large structure by old Park City standards, it has stood at the southeast corner of Heber Avenue and Park Avenue since before the turn of the 20th century.

At one time, before Maurine bought the property, it was the home of a young Willis W. Ritter. A non-Mormon, Ritter would go on to become a federal judge whom the dominant culture of Utah found repugnant. He was the last of a string of federal judges whose main task was to remind Utah that it, too, was in America.

Ritter was brilliant but unorthodox. The 10th Circuit Court of Appeals often reversed his decisions, but in every case that eventually reached the U.S. Supreme Court, his original decisions were found proper.

When Maurine owned the building there was a large sign that read, "Foster's Home Cooked Meals." You couldn't miss it as you turned off Park Avenue going toward Main Street, yet the sign did little to help her business. Perhaps word of mouth traveled faster.

Ma Foster's lacked the décor of a café. There were none of the behind-the-counter items for sale that were so prevalent in restaurants of that era. A cigar box took the place of a cash register. And the small dining room made it feel more like a private home than a public restaurant.

There were four small tables with mismatched chairs. Though it was lighted well enough, the restaurant still felt dark and dingy.

Any time I went to Maurine's restaurant it was with Wayne Putman. Wayne, a high school classmate, was streetwise and on a first-name basis with every character in the camp. He usually knew where the action was.

Maurine's coffee could rival any for its clout. Her volume of sales was so slight that the coffee stewed in the pot, building

A sign advertises Maurine Foster's home-cooked meals in this early 1950s parade photograph. This 1890s building still stands on the southeast corner of Park and Heber Avenues. *Photo courtesy of the Kendall Webb Collection, Park City Museum.*

strength with each passing hour. We would sit there, nursing a cup of that coffee that neither of us wanted, and smoke. No one reprimanded us and we felt quite grown up.

Like everything else in Park City during the 1950s, boardinghouses fell on hard times. Maurine was forced to try something different.

"God knows, I've tried selling food and they don't want that," I overheard her say in Thompson's grocery store. "I'll have to sell them what they want." A short time later I would discover what she was selling.

I used to take a shortcut to and from Main Street that ran behind Foster's, across the lots that now house the Fashion Coalition Building and the Park Hotel. Late at night on March 9, 1953, I was on my way home from the Egyptian Theatre. The snow was hard-packed on the path, but as you reached Park Avenue there was a huge bank where it had been plowed off the street. As you climbed over the bank, it would seem to anyone watching from Park Avenue that you had come down the back outside staircase from Maurine's.

As I emerged onto Park Avenue that night, I was blinded by a powerful spotlight. Suddenly two of the biggest plainclothes cops I've seen pounced on me and shoved me into the backseat of a parked car.

The idiots were convinced that I had just left Maurine's. I showed them the well-used shortcut that they should have known about. Finally Roy Howard showed up and vouched for me.

Roy was a native of Park City who worked as a crime photographer and at any other job he could find. Years later he disappeared. They found his car east of Park City in the area we called the Big Four. The key was in the ignition, the doors were open, but no Roy.

It was rumored that the Feds were about to issue a warrant for his arrest for misusing the U.S. Mail. The talk was that he was using his photographic talents for pornographic purposes. For a long time we would speculate whether he took flight or someone "took him out." Anyway, I will always be grateful that he stepped forward that night and vouched for me.

I was given a warning to keep quiet about what was happening and sent home. I watched the slowly developing raid from my front porch. I really couldn't detect much, just headlights, red spotlights, the occasional beam of a flashlight, shadowy figures moving back and forth, and muffled conversation. Many people believed the law cracked down on Maurine because she operated her house of ill-repute in the Park City business district instead of on "the line" (a string of houses on Heber Avenue at the mouth of Deer Valley).

In Maurine's defense this would have been next to impossible. It seemed that, as business dropped off and these shacks became vacant, there would be fires, the cause always mysterious. Once someone tried his hand with dynamite. The good citizens always chalked it up to youthful excesses until only Bessie Wheeler's house remained.

Bessie must have set some sort of longevity record for running a house of prostitution in the same location. Year after year her blue house kept the red porch light glowing. And generation after generation of adolescent boys would try their best to steal that red light. Some succeeded; most did not.

On my best try I unscrewed the light until it went out, but by then my fingers were burned and a couple of cowboy types from our farm belt came charging out from the parlor. They probably didn't have their boots on because they didn't give much of a chase. Then again they most likely had a better sport on their minds.

All the red-light-district operators kept low profiles. Their girls were never allowed out on the town. They were transported into and out of town by yellow cabs from Salt Lake. In fact, until the ski boom began, I doubt if a single person ever came to Park City by taxi who was not connected to the trade. Even now, when I see a taxi from Salt Lake, my first thought is, "Where are the hookers going?"

The old-time operators like Bessie recognized the expenses of doing business. There were payoffs, yes, but more important were the small things they did to build goodwill. The anonymous box of groceries sent to a poor widow; a boy sent on a Scout outing; flowers at an indigent's funeral. All done quietly, yet so all would know. They did it well in Park City.

None of these houses were fancy or high class. They would be termed workingmen's parlors, five-dollar houses. The five-dollar

Bessie Wheeler's house was the last one standing on "The Line," Park City's red-light district. *Photo courtesy of the Kendall Webb Collection, Park City Museum.*

price was cast in concrete. I don't think it changed in the lifetime of most miners.

Since there was only one house remaining on the line – the one occupied by Bessie – Maurine was forced to try a new area after the 1953 raid. She set up shop on the lower end of Easy Street, an unmaintained rut of a road that paralleled Poison Creek below Heber Avenue. Many old-timers and winos lived in shacks along the banks of the creek on Easy Street.

Maurine's business thrived in its new location. At that time I was working after school and weekends in a gas station, and hardly a day would go by that I didn't give directions to her house or Bessie Wheeler's.

Sometimes, if it was near closing time at the service station and some party would ask for directions to the cat house, I would send him on a wild goose chase, usually to some prominent citizen's home. The town marshal or high school principal was often the target of my juvenile humor. I don't know if any of the "sporting men" ever tried the houses I sent them to. I never waited around for feedback.

One Friday night in the autumn of 1954 my group threw a beer bash to celebrate some now-forgotten date, perhaps simply the fact that it was Friday.

Fortified with beer, we descended on Maurine's house, each depending on the courage of the group to back him up. I was in the forefront, boisterous, loud, showing my guts. If the truth were known, I didn't see Maurine's car and was convinced there was no one home.

My mistake. The door swung open and Maurine's vast frame filled the doorway until little light could escape from within. She singled me out of the crowd and let loose with a tongue-lashing I would never forget.

"God damn you, Gary Kimball. If your mother knew you were here she would be down here playing Carrie Nation with an ax in hand. Now get your little ass out of here and take your friends with you."

I had no idea Maurine knew who I was, let alone my name. Back in those days, when the town was still a community, most everybody greeted everyone on the street. But with Maurine the best you could hope for was a grunt. She didn't waste pleasantries on snotty-nose kids, even when she poured your coffee at the restaurant.

Anyway, I was highly embarrassed that night and subjected to a lot of good-natured kidding from my friends for quite a while.

Maurine's house on Easy Street did not last long. Sheriff George Fisher raided her establishment early in December 1954 and closed her down. She never reopened.

There was some speculation as to why she was singled out. Some say she was arrested to appease the new county attorney,

Morgan Lewis, who was clamoring for action. Others suspected that Bessie Wheeler brought pressure on the sheriff to eliminate competition in a dwindling economy. The joke that went around was, "She was just too big of a target."

Maurine suffered a heart attack in the autumn of 1955. After convalescing in the Miners Hospital for several weeks she was taken to Salt Lake City by ambulance. There she boarded a train for her sister's home in California.

After that, times were a little harder on Easy Street.

Webb's World

Much of Webb's income was derived from school activities such as sporting events. Most parents would buy a half-dozen prints of their son performing a slam dunk or scoring a touchdown. Some activities were less spectacular. Still, parents loved them. This photo shows the author and Viola Williams Sanchez dancing their promenade. For several mornings before school each week, Nan McPolin, the girls' P.E. instructor, would teach the junior class this dance. For some of the boys it was a grueling experience. *Photo courtesy of the Kimball Archive.*

The first time I heard of Kendall Webb was over the dinner table from my excited older brother, Paul. He and his friend, Bob Cullen, had heard about a strange man who was opening a shop on Main Street and had plans to start a Scout troop.

After school they stopped at his shop and found the man cooking bacon. He had wrapped the bacon around a long poker, removed the lid of a potbelly stove and was roasting it over an open flame. Smoke was pouring out into the room. It was like camping out at home.

Paul couldn't wait to join his Scout troop. I discovered that, at age 10, I was too young to get in, confirming that life was unfair.

In 1946 Webb opened the last new business to appear on Main Street for many years to come. And, of all things, he opened a photo studio.

Though a poor livelihood, photography was a passion for Kendall Webb. A West Virginian, he moved to Utah shortly after World War II and, with a partner, Murri Hair, opened the Valley Studio in Midway, Utah, in 1945. After 18 months and a pile of debts, they looked for cheaper rent and discovered Park City. They kept the name Valley Studio because they had already printed stationery and receipt books, though they would be the first to admit that it did not fit their new surroundings. It was not long before Hair quit, giving his share of the business to Webb.

Webb rented a building at 401 Main Street until 1953, when he bought the old Taylor building at 523 Main. In the mid-1960s he erected a building on the next lot to the north (now the Main Street Deli). The front of the building he rented to Dr. John O. Lambert for his dentist office; the back he used as a studio. A blue screen served as a background for a huge ancient portrait camera.

During the Depression, Webb had served an apprenticeship as a steam-fitter, but work was scarce. He finally found a job at Pearl Harbor, Hawaii, about 1940. There he settled in, started a Scout troop and pursued his hobby of photography.

Webb told the most remarkable – perhaps unbelievable – story about December 7, 1941, and the Japanese bombing of Pearl Harbor. That weekend, he said, he had taken his Scout troop on a bus excursion. Not knowing that the island was under attack, he said, they paid little attention to the low-flying aircraft they saw. In hindsight, he was sure that the bus had been strafed by a Japanese plane. He recalled that you could see the dust jumping along the side of the road and that the bus driver looked over to him and muttered, "Sure is a lot of grasshoppers out there."

When he returned to Pearl, the authorities would not let him in. The lax security of peacetime that allowed him to leave the shipyard without his identification card (and money) was now wartime tight! It was three days of sleeping on the beach before he was readmitted to the base. He returned to the mainland on the first available transportation, worked in defense industries in Arizona until war's end, then moved to Utah.

Webb was the biggest eater I have ever known. He could consume more food at one sitting than most people could eat in a week.

Once he shared a Thanksgiving dinner at my home. On refusing another piece of pumpkin pie, he explained, "No, I've got to save some room. I've been invited down to Coach Reeves's house for dinner at six o'clock."

"You've got to be kidding," my dad responded, knowing that Webb had already eaten double or triple portions of every dish on the table.

"No. In fact, I ate up at Ernest Lange's place before I came here."

Few people could hold their own with Webb at the table. But when necessary he could fast. I know of one occasion when he was camping and a pack containing his food was lost. He would chew up a bullion cube, wash it down with a canteen of water and claim he had had soup for supper.

Webb joined the Park City Kiwanis Club and convinced the club to sponsor a Scout troop. In February of 1947 the Kiwanis Club organized Troop 162 with Albert Williams as Scoutmaster and Ken

Webb as assistant Scoutmaster. Williams lasted only a few months and was happy to turn the job over to Webb.

There had been Scouting in Park City's past, but no troop had been active for years. The Mormon First Ward still had its charter for Troup 169 and claimed to be the founders of Park City Scouting. But it was a claim true only on paper. The Veterans War Memorial Building on Main Street had a Scout room that had gathered dust for years. Its walls were covered in log strips to simulate a log cabin. There was a small stage for conducting ceremonies and a large closet to store flags and camping gear.

To his Scouts, Kendall Webb was known simply as Webb. I believe I was in my late teens before I learned his first name. His troop was so successful that, before long, other community organizations wanted troops of their own. The Elks Club was granted a charter for Troop 448 and the Mormon Church reactivated Troop 169.

All the troops were invited on the bus camping tours that Webb planned and organized. Usually they lasted a week. There were few scenic locations in the West where he did not take his Scouts – Canada to Mexico, California to Colorado. They were great adventures for boys for whom leaving the city limits was a novel idea.

Webb loved camping and river running, and with his quiet sense of humor he was an ideal companion for this type of outing. One afternoon, shortly after I was discharged from the Navy, he called me into his store and asked if I wanted to go on a week river trip through Glen Canyon on the Colorado River. They were leaving that afternoon, but because of a cancellation there was room for me.

Before rushing home to get my camping gear, I asked Webb who was sponsoring the trip. "Socottwa," he told me. I assumed the organization had adapted some sort of Indian name that reflected its activities.

In the last few minutes, while we waited for the bus, I dashed to the Central Drug Store and purchased a carton of cigarettes and several condoms from Doc Gordon. Using an old boatswain trick from the Navy, I rolled a condom over the carton of cigarettes, thus insuring they would keep dry in the roughest water.

I was pleased with my cleverness; I now knew my time in the Navy was not a complete loss. I delighted in showing nearly everyone on the trip this clever invention and told them to feel free to apply it to their own gear. Webb just smiled.

I believe it was on the fourth day out, on a Sunday, during religious services, that I discovered what Socottwa stood for: South Cottonwood Ward. It was a Mormon river-running organization! I could have crawled under a rock.

I asked Webb why he didn't tell me. His reply: "Y'all didn't ask." Damn, though, his eyes could dance.

Webb was popular with his Scouts because he accepted them as peers; he never talked down to them and would listen to their complaints or stories with undivided attention.

Some of his Scouts were outstanding. Bob Mawhinney became the youngest Scout in America to achieve the rank of Eagle. Since then the age of admission has been lowered from 12 to 11 and his record didn't stand long.

Webb recruited Howard Coleman, the only African-American boy in Park City, into his troop. Living in Park City was hard on young Howard; many young whites would hassle him. But we didn't dare show bigotry in Webb's troop. Howard was an outstanding Scout and good with a camera. Webb taught him how to develop film and gave him the use of his darkroom. Later, Howard would become a professional photographer in the Marine Corps.

Unfortunately, Webb's Southern vocabulary didn't include the word "negro". One afternoon Webb saw me passing his shop and called me in. He told me the fireside meeting planned for that night at Lake Flats had been changed to Nigger Hollow and asked me to pass the word to several boys in my neighborhood, Howard being one of them.

I did okay until I got to Howard's house. At age twelve I did not recognize any difference between negro and nigger, but I knew one was in bad form, and I was not about to say either word to Howard. So I acted dumb, pretending I couldn't remember the name. I played charades, pointing, mumbling, and trying to act out where we were supposed to meet. Finally, Howard said, "We're meeting in Nigger Hollow, ain't we?" I nodded in relief and he went into his house, laughing so hard you could still hear him even after the door was shut.

I can remember Webb losing his temper only once. On the Glen Canyon river trip we were walking up Forbidden Canyon to Rainbow Bridge. Some Scouts were using willow sticks as whips to kill the many lizards that were sunning themselves on the narrow canyon walls.

Webb tolerated this for about 20 minutes, perhaps waiting for the Scouts' own leaders to end the mayhem. When no one did anything to end the killing, Webb blew up. He turned beet red and gave the boys a tongue-lashing that may still be burning their ears. If Webb had had the power, those boys would have been drummed out of the Scouts.

As far as I know, Webb was a self-taught photographer. His main income came from weddings and the high school annual yearbook. When taking yearbook photos, he would bring a spare necktie for the boys who failed to dress for the occasion. There would be page after page of photos of male students, all with the same necktie. For many, it was the only tie they had ever worn.

He never missed a high school sporting event. The photo of a player dunking a basketball or making a tackle always brought the proud parents into his shop to buy photos of their son, the star.

Once, in 1964, Webb wanted to know if I had ever been audited by the federal government for taxes. I told him no, but wondered why he'd asked. He nodded over his shoulder and I could see someone bent over, looking into a filing cabined. The IRS was upon him!

Webb told me that he always sent in his signed tax form, but instead of filling it out he would write in bold print across it, "Didn't Make Enough!" It had satisfied the government for over a decade; he wondered why they were kicking up a storm now.

Webb had all his records. They were in no particular order, but he had every scrap of paper that related to his business. The agent pored over his records for three days, then left, muttering to himself, never to return. Webb's only remark was, "I told them I didn't make enough."

Webb developed the form of lung cancer that comes from working around asbestos, probably caused by his work as a steam-fitter at Pearl Harbor. In 1975 he put his affairs in order and sold his photo shop to Nick Nass with the understanding that Nass would keep the photo shop open.

Nass kept his promise and operated the Main Street Photographer from Webb's old building at 573 Main for many years. The photographs that accompany this story come from Webb's collection, now located at the Park City Museum.

Webb died at age 68 on June 19, 1975, and is buried in his family plot in Huntington, West Virginia.

Club Rules

This photo, taken for tax-assessment purposes, shows The Club (the narrow building with the BEER sign) in the 1950s. In 1978, a mirror image was built on the uphill lot previously occupied by Tessman's radio and small appliance shop.
PCHS tax photo, courtesy of the Park City Museum.

I remember the time I first tried to buy a beer in Heine's Club. I was sixteen and had been buying cigarettes there for over a year. On this night my friend Tom Daly and I were elected to go in for a beer.

I don't recall why we decided to try The Club. Perhaps the Law was watching the other tavern we used, or maybe things were so loose that we thought we could double the number of bars that would serve us.

Tom did the talking. "Give us a case of Coors to go."

"Are you of age?" Heine quietly asked from behind the bar.

"You're goddamn right we are!" answered a swelled-out Tom.

"Good. Then go up to The Oak for it," replied Heine as he turned his back on us and slowly walked to the other end of the bar. I can still feel the snickers of several customers as we made our retreat.

I was out of the Navy and of age before I ordered another beer in The Club.

In hindsight I'm quite sure we could have gotten the beer if we had given Heine our right ages and had been a little humble upon ordering it.

If you were to line up a thousand people, in all different occupations, you would pick out Heine Hernon as the bartender. He just looked the part. A short, squatty man – the spitting image of J. Edgar Hoover – he always wore a white shirt and tie and a white bar apron tied at his waist. He often wore an old button-style maroon sweater.

Heine was soft-spoken and always a gentleman; I don't remember him ever raising his voice, yet he was always in total control of his establishment. Today he could have been a skilled clinical psychologist. Heine had class.

After a brief career at Iowa Copper (a mine between Park City and Brighton), he became the chief mechanic at Park City's King Con Mine. Then he accepted employment in The Club, 449 Main Street, owned and operated by Louis Dunn. When Dunn moved to Ely, Nevada, to be near his family in the early 1930s, Heine took over the ownership.

In those days The Club was tiny. The building, though two stories tall, was only twelve feet wide. The second story at one time was used as a card parlor, but after Heine raised his family and his wife died, it became his living quarters.

A large portion of the main floor space was lost to the wide staircase heading upstairs, but what remained was elegant in a quaint sort of way. Patent-leather wainscoting lined the walls to four feet in height. Several large elk heads adorned the walls. The ceiling was covered in a pressed tin cinquefoil pattern that was popular around the turn of the 20th century. There were only two ceiling lights, large white porcelain acorn-shaped globes hanging from five-foot chains.

The bar stretched across the north side of the building. There were no bar stools. The back bar, built of solid oak, stood nine feet high. High in the center a circular mirror studied the customers. The patrons, in return, studied themselves in two massive mirrors that flanked narrow stained-glass panels. All were French beveled. Built-in cabinets at both ends had identical stained-glass doors.

Directly west of the bar stood the tavern's only source of heat: an oil-fed parlor stove constructed of brown pressed steel. Here too was Heine's only modern convenience, a color console television set. The shelf that housed the cathedral-style radio was now of lesser importance.

Heine was addicted to baseball. As far as I know, the only time the television or radio was turned on was for a baseball game. There was no juke box.

The single restroom in the tavern was the main reason Heine barred females. Actually, he didn't completely bar them, for I've met many a woman who boasted of the time she was in The Club. And then there was a certain clique of regulars known as the Merry Widows. I guess it boiled down to who the woman was, and the status of her male escort.

I remember stopping in The Club one Labor Day with a date. After some time my date went to the restroom. In a moment she returned, stating, "I can't go in there. There's only one restroom and there's no door!"

Heine was serving a table close to ours and overheard her plight. He motioned with his head toward the restroom and said, "Go ahead."

"I can't," she said. It was more of a plea than a statement.

"It will be okay. Come on."

He led her through the crowded bar. There, at the restroom doorway, Heine stood guard, arms folded over his chest, feet planted. It was French General Robert Nivelle's classic pose: "They shall not pass."

Over the cash register Heine had driven a sixteen-penny nail, cut off its head and filed it to a sharp point. For years that nail received all the paper currency the business took in. To show his support for the mines and miners, Heine favored silver currency and would not soil his cash register with vile paper money.

Years later, when forced to give up this practice under threat of a lawsuit for defacing U.S. currency, Heine still refused to put the vile stuff in his cash register; instead, he would leave it on top of the machine.

I don't know what he did with his money after closing time. I know he didn't keep it in the safe, for he reserved his safe for true treasures – his cheese and crackers.

At closing time those patrons who did not take heed and leave would be locked in until the newspaper was delivered in the morning. Heine paid the tab. It was at this time that he brought out his best booze and opened his safe for the prized cheese and crackers. I've always regretted missing out on those lock-ins.

Utah went dry on the first day of August, 1917, two years before federal Prohibition took effect. For these first years, quality whiskey was smuggled in from Wyoming, and in time any good booze became known as Wyoming whiskey. The Club used a unique system for delivery of the contraband.

At the back of The Club two long lodge poles ran up from the second-story door to the edge of Park Avenue. This would be about a forty-degree slope running from the street to the tavern, a distance of about fifty feet. They would roll the barrels down this makeshift ramp. Although the barrels traveled at an astounding speed, seldom were there accidents. The local police must have known about this system, but no move was ever made to stop it.

There were many other stories about the elaborate measures that Dunn and Heine took during Prohibition. It's said that they installed a partition, suspended by weights, under a second-story window in The Club. If raided, they would roll the barrels of booze against the partitions, which lifted from the pressure, and the booze would come to rest in the attic of the adjacent single-story building. I never understood the mechanics of this operation, or can even vouch for its existence. Heine never talked of it in my presence.

Heine seldom sold beer by the case to take out, for it would have been warm, and that was against his principles, even though The Club itself did not have refrigeration. I guess I drank beer there for several years before I discovered that fact. And yet no bar in the camp served a colder bottle of beer.

The method he used was simple. He would fill the sink with bottles and leave the cold-water tap cracked open. His volume of sales was slow enough that each and every beer was as cold as Park City drinking water which, during the 1950s, was so cold you could get an ice-cream headache by drinking it. Only on the Fourth of July and Labor Day would Heine buy a few three-hundred-pound blocks of ice to cope with the increased volume of sales.

The Club had class because Heine had class. Today, when you order a bottle of beer, the bartender will ask if you want a glass, but his tone is often so intimidating that the drinker refuses, not wanting to upset his host. With Heine there was no choice. Beer was meant to be consumed by the glass, and he insisted on pouring the first one. He tilted the glass just so, and poured oh so slowly to develop the proper head of foam. Only when it met with his approval would he turn the glass over to the customer.

Heine kept the price for small bottles of Coke and 7-Up at five cents for years after everyone else had raised it to ten. When asked about this he would only say, "Damned stuff ain't worth more."

I suspect that by today's standards The Club would have rated low. It was dingy, smoke-filled, with no music, little seating and a limited choice of beverages. And yet, on occasion, the Who's Who of Utah would gather there. A federal judge, a Utah Supreme Court judge, a state tax commissioner, a state senator, and several mining men of great wealth and power would mingle with the dregs of the camp, all on equal terms.

As time passed and the old mining camp slowed in the late 1950s and early '60s, The Club slowed too. It seemed as though Heine spent the last years of his life looking forlornly out the front window of his establishment, perhaps wondering and dreaming of when the good times would return.

Heine died on February 13, 1970. But the advent of skiing brought new prosperity to The Club. In 1978 a mirror-image addition was built to the south where Tessman's Radio and Small Appliance shop once stood, and the entire structure was remodeled about five years later. The Club continued to attract a loyal following for a while, but the building was later converted into an art gallery. At this writing (in 2022) it houses Annex Burger.

The Hidden Life of a Miner

Bill Neil and Cappy Roach tending bar at The Oak in 1957.
Photo courtesy of the Kendall Webb Collection, Park City Museum.

In 1902 an ad appeared in *The Park Record* declaring The Oak to be "Park City's newest and best equipped saloon." Fifty-four years later, another ad proclaimed: "The Oak, Park City's oldest established business." Between these two advertisements lies the story of early Park City's best known, most popular saloon.

The Oak was somewhat akin to a community center. There was no stigma of evil lurking behind its doors. At times it was awash with kids selling empty soda-pop and beer bottles for a penny apiece, and then buying candy or a soda with their newly acquired wealth. It was an emporium of sorts, carrying a full line of candy, cigarettes, cigars, ice cream, handkerchiefs, Band-Aids,

Bromo-Seltzer, smoked-salmon strips, dried salted shrimp, hard-boiled eggs, pickled eggs, dill pickles, punchboards and their prizes, beef jerky, snuff, chewing tobacco, combs, writing paper, envelopes, pens, and – yes – you could even get beer.

The Oak first opened its doors on November 15, 1902. Located at 415 Main Street, The Oak was in a large two-story building built by Henry Spriggs and another man named Prior.

It was said that Henry Spriggs was Park City's answer to Diamond Jim Brady. His large gold watch and chain, along with his huge handlebar mustache, set him apart from the crowd. The loud checkered patterns of his suits denoted him, by Park City standards, as a man of means.

Too, Spriggs was a man proud of his physical ability. In 1910, at age sixty, he bet $100 that he could walk from The Oak to the Rio Grande Depot in Salt Lake City in only seven hours. Unfortunately, he slightly miscalculated. When his time ran out he still had a mile and a half to go.

The most senior bartender I knew in The Oak was Bill Neil. Bill loved to tell stories about The Oak's early days. At times he would laugh so hard at his stories that his tears would blur his vision.

Bill Neil was a large man, about six feet. But his powerful frame had withered with the passing of the years. What hair he had was gray. His ears protruded at a near right angle and often he would cup a hand to his left ear to amplify his hearing. Bill had seen extensive combat in World War I and his hearing was damaged as a result. His lungs had been burned by mustard gas so he abstained from smoking. But he did enjoy a glass in the company of friends.

Bill loved to tell about the coming of Prohibition to Utah, and the frenzy on the last day of July in 1917. The Oak patrons hurried to consume every last drop of alcohol on the premises before Bill Gidley, the city sexton, could make his way up Main Street ringing his gravedigger's bell to proclaim the good times gone forever.

But lo and behold, at the stroke of midnight, when management went to lock the door of The Oak, no key could be found. The doors had not been locked since the saloon first opened in 1902. The state would have to wait one extra day to lock The Oak.

Another story Bill delighted in telling was about The Oak's practice of covering the floors with sawdust years after more modern establishments had ceased doing the same. The occasional tourist who wandered into the place could not resist asking how often The Oak changed the sawdust.

The standard answer was, "Sawdust, hell! That's last night's furniture!" Bill would have to wipe the tears from his eyes as he told his tales.

Another legendary bartender was an Englishman, Les Roach, known to all as Cappy. He was a small man – about five foot four – and his slight frame had slipped with the years. Cappy's perpetually red nose would glow at times toward the end of the evening. This was the only indication that the contents of his beer glass were ever consumed. By nature he was a quiet man. He did enjoy a good laugh, but his humor was very subtle.

Cappy rolled his own smokes using Prince Albert pipe tobacco and a brown wheat-germ paper. The end result looked primitive, but the odor was pleasant.

Upon entering The Oak through the double set of swinging doors, you would find, on the left, a solid oak bar about 30 feet in length. However, the massive back-bar didn't live up to The Oak's name – it was stained mahogany. The large mirrors were flanked by two great columns with deep-cut scroll work.

At the center of the bar a removable grate marred the flat surface, but this grate housed the secret to the coldest draft beer in the entire state. The grate covered an eight-inch-diameter pipe that ran to the basement. Inside this pipe were hundreds of feet of coiled copper tubing that carried beer from a keg in the basement to the spigot behind the bar. This eight-inch pipe was kept packed with ice cubes. Every so often the bartender would remove the grate and dump ice by the bucket down the pipe, thus ensuring the coldest of cold beer.

By the late 1950s The Oak had seen better days. It was dingy in appearance. The benches that hugged the walls hid the dark-stained wainscoting. But the classic brass spittoons, rapidly vanishing elsewhere, were still in place along the bar.

High on the back wall, obscured by paneling, a large steel "bird cage" still hung suspended from the saloon's ceiling which a man could crawl into from the floor above.

Early on Friday morning, April 22, 1910, two men robbed The Oak. Lining customers up along the brass rail, one of the outlaws proclaimed, "I'm Kid Parker! If you want to live, put up your hands and be fast about it!"

While his partner covered the crowd, he went down the line of miners, taking all their valuables, and then proceeded to take the gold and silver coins from the roulette and faro tables. Disappointed with the take, the "Kid" warned those present, "We don't like this, and we will call on you again in six months!"

When this holdup took place, George Leroy Parker, alias Butch Cassidy, was still running the Wild Bunch gang. Some of his close associates called him Kid Parker and it's known that some toughs adopted the name to give them more bravado.

Illustration by Harley Campos.

Henry Spriggs, taking the threat of a return visit seriously, suspended the "bird cage" from the ceiling and kept a shotgun guard in it whenever his gaming tables had good play.

West of The Oak's five booths stood the billiard tables. The two regulation pool tables got little play. But the third table was something. It was a mammoth "Life" table that, with its tight pockets, either hooked or cured the novice in short order.

To this day I have never seen the billiard game of Life played. I'm sure that somewhere there are people who know the rules and actually play the game. But a Life table is so grand that its own game does not need to be played. Any other pool game played on a Life table becomes not just a game but an experience to retell to your grandchildren in your waning years.

Bottle pool and pea pool were popular, but the game that got the most attention, and was played for hours each day, year in and year out, was snooker. The house charged ten cents per player per game.

I was too young to see some of the great players like Ed Jenkins, who racked balls in The Oak for years. He went on to become renowned as a photographer and leading local restaurateur known to all as Pop Jenks. But I'm satisfied with the caliber of play I witnessed.

Watching Frank Nancarrow play gave "English" a new meaning; his game was near perfect grammatically. Harvey Gonzales was master of the straight stick. These two played many a series where the table stakes were pegged at over two hundred dollars a game. Two thousand dollars could change hands in a night, more than a year's wages to most of the spectators.

There also were several pinball machines in The Oak and, like those in all the Park City taverns, they paid off in cash. There were certain people who schemed to beat these machines by means that were not considered legal. They would use magnets, or would drill holes and try to manipulate the ball with a thin stiff wire. Usually these patrons were caught within minutes and sent on their way. But the amazing thing to me was Cappy Roach's unfailingly forgiving nature. He usually allowed the culprits back within a day or two.

One trick that had me puzzled for years involved a tiny pinpoint hole placed in the glass covering the pinball machine. How could a person drill a hole in glass?

Recently one of the culprits explained to me how it was done. They would take a small piece of dry ice and freeze the precise spot on the glass where they wanted the hole. Then they would take a small steel ball bearing and, from a height of about four inches, drop it on that spot. Bingo – a hole so small an ant would have had a hard time fitting through and only a skilled eye could locate.

It was said that, when Prohibition came to Park City, 20 saloons closed down that night. The next morning 20 "soft-drink parlors" opened up. Nineteen of them were doing business as usual. The Oak, however, played it straight and became a true ice-cream and soft-drink parlor.

When Prohibition ended in 1933, The Oak resumed its place as the leading saloon in the camp, but it had a hard time forsaking its youthful customers. The Oak became what would best be described as a family saloon. The management never knowingly sold beer to minors, but if they wanted a soft drink or a malt they were welcome.

And, if you tried their Chase-brand ice cream, you would know why it was in demand. Many of the most saintly of the Mormon community would brave the public ridicule to savor its flavor. Cappy would hand pack it until the carton was nearly bursting at the seams and the top lid flaps bulged open.

And oh, the malts they made – thick, with such a rich flavor. The vanilla malts were always served with a shaker of nutmeg in case the customer wanted to add more. I once remarked to Cappy that sprinkling nutmeg on a malt was a strange custom, and that I didn't know of any malt shop that did the same. His only comment was, "Yes, it sure is strange that they don't serve them proper."

Cappy made chocolate malts with chocolate ice cream and strawberry malts with strawberry ice cream, which was the extent of the flavors he carried. Often, all he had on hand was vanilla. If that was the case, then there would be no chocolate or strawberry malts. Cappy refused to substitute a flavoring syrup for the real thing.

But the customers were what gave The Oak its real flavor. One of the lunch-bucket brigade whom I particularly liked was Pat Terry. When he got off shift from the mine at the end of the day, he would start at the bottom of Main Street and gradually work his way home – stopping, of course, at each saloon along the way.

Pat was famous for his son-of-a-bitch stories. If you heard one, you would know what the name meant. And his ability to coin a phrase or pigeonhole a character would rival a Damon Runyon. I know that I always came up on the short end when jesting with him.

Once, when I was trying to impress him with my worldliness by telling him about some experience of mine during my tour with the Navy, he cut me short with, "Son-of-a-bitch, Kimball, you don't know what you're talking about. Why, I've been in more cities than you've been in grocery stores."

At that time I was operating a small corner grocery store. I sputtered into silence. But it was hard to get mad at Pat. His delivery was always punctuated with a smile and a twinkle of the eyes.

One couple who frequented The Oak was Cowboy (Jim) and Clara Clausen. Jim looked like Hopalong Cassidy sidekick California Carlson, but he always dressed in bib overalls and looked more like a railroad engineer. The Clausens were both slight in stature and, while addressing one another, used a vernacular that was shocking to those who didn't know them. To lessen the sting, each parley began and ended with an affectionate term of love.

"Oh Clara, you sweet honey of a thing you, that was the poorest damned excuse for laundry you did today. What did you do, get the scrub water out of Poison Creek like a dumb whore, my sugar pie baby?"

"My dear old Cowboy darling, my laundry would look a helluva lot better if you'd stop shitting your pants, you old petunia bum."

They would keep up this kind of patter all night, and at times they would actually hold hands. Ah, the sweet mysteries of love.

Another couple who visited The Oak at times was Red Spencer and his wife Virginia. Both were short and pudgy and in their fifties. She wore glasses as thick as the bottom of a Coke bottle. Red

The Oak (on the left) as it looked in this 1957 Labor Day parade photograph.
Photo courtesy of the Kendall Webb Collection, Park City Museum.

would often carry a pint whiskey bottle, and if you happened to bump into him in the restroom he would offer you a shot. If you were all set for the naked bite of raw bourbon, it would be a shock to find the distinct dry flavor of chokecherry wine trickling down your throat. Red made a wine that he was so proud of that he liked to keep a sample on hand.

Before the evening was over Red would talk someone into asking – or coaxing – his wife to yodel. At first she would refuse, but in time she would give in. Now, I'm no authority on the art of yodeling, but I think she would rank with the best of them. And Red would be standing at the back of the crowd, a look of pride on his face and tears glittering in his eyes.

Once character I found fascinating was Drawbar (Bill) Jones. He was in his late fifties and wore an oversized World War I trench coat that draped to his feet. He had spent his early years in the border patrol in the Southwest and many years in the Navy. His tales about China and the Great White Fleet were fascinating.

Drawbar had one gimmick – or challenge – that I never took him up on. His standing offer was that, for each beer you bought him, he would show you a new tattoo. Even with beer at ten cents a glass, I didn't know many people who could afford to see all of his tattoos.

The Oak, like all taverns in Park City, charged ten cents a glass for draft beer and twenty-five cents for bottled beer. They carried every major brand of beer, but Coors was the majority choice, except in the spring.

Sometime around March or April Becker's brewery would distribute its famous bock beer. I still remember its ad, "Becker's Bock is Back." It was heralded as some sort of spring tonic that would cure all your ills. All the old-timers would have a bottle or two and rave about it – just enough to sucker us novice drinkers into joining in. Then they would quietly switch back to Coors.

Becker's Bock was rich, dark in color, and had a sweet, somewhat pungent flavor. Most novices would drink it all evening. Then, sometime during the night, they would discover how powerful a tonic Becker's Bock was. Diarrhea! This brew certainly flushed the system clean. It was a mean joke but, once I was initiated, I couldn't wait to play it on someone else.

Back then every saloon established its own style to fit in with the community or its ethnic customers. These styles became traditions and, at times, even legends. The Oak had a style and a management completely loyal to the mines and miners. The silver-mining economy was the saloon's bread and butter, and The Oak paid it more than lip service. Management loved to give out silver currency for change.

For example, if you went into The Oak, ordered a ten-cent draft beer and gave them a five-dollar bill, your change would come back as four silver dollars, one half dollar, one quarter, one dime and one nickel. All would be silver except the nickel, which was usually a World War II nickel with high silver content.

Now, a pocketful of silver dollars could be bothersome if you had a long way to walk or were dancing or doing some other physical activity. They could actually wear your hide raw where they came in contact. That's a problem I wish I could once more complain about.

But you never wanted to ask Cappy to exchange your silver cartwheels for paper currency. He didn't get angry or anything; in fact, he was always very pleasant, but firm. If pressed, his answer would go like, "No, we don't do that here."

"You got to be kidding. I know you got plenty of dollar bills."

"Our business is taking paper money out of circulation, not putting it in."

"Well hell, Cappy, it won't hurt you this once, will it?"

"No, I'm sorry, but that's not the way we do things here."

Cappy would smile and walk to the other end of the bar, leaving you feeling foolish and a little embarrassed that you had made such an asinine request.

In the early 1960s, changes were taking place in Park City. The mining-based economy that had always been the camp lifeblood was in a decade-long slump. The ski industry was beginning to shape a new course for the community. But The Oak somehow missed out on the growth.

As the pace at The Oak slowed, there were many nights when the place was empty except for Cappy and his lady friend Mildred sitting at the end of the bar. At times their quiet talk was punctuated by soft laughter – private jokes that are now lost.

Then, in 1965, the heirs of Henry Spriggs shocked the community by giving a lease on The Oak to Max Rasmussen. Max went into The Oak on a grand scale, with new booths, tables, chairs and stools. He splashed new paint and carpet throughout the building.

A new beginning? Hardly. It was, instead, a sad ending. Max had done it all on credit. Without fanfare, the creditors removed those new bright chrome fixtures, rolled up the carpet and padlocked the doors within a week of his opening.

Max himself had already left town.

About the time this happened, I bumped into Cappy at the Post Office and offered my sympathy for what I considered the shabby treatment he had received. He replied, "You don't think 53 years was enough? I'm glad to be rid of it." Perhaps I'm wrong, but I think his acceptance masked other feelings.

Several others attempted to run a saloon at this location before it became a women's apparel shop. In August 1973 the building burned down during the last big fire on Main Street. Fittingly enough, the property is now a small park where you can sit and relax and enjoy a few moments of peace.

Low Wages and Cold Feet

and the Brief but Glorious Struggles of the Park City Lift Operators' Union

The author (left) loads skiers onto the Treasure Mountains J-bar lift, which was built in the Judge Mine machine shop. *Photo courtesy of the Kimball Archive.*

Back in December of 1965 I got a job as a lift operator at the Treasure Mountains ski resort. What happened that day wasn't my fault – hell, someone could have given me a few instructions or training, but they just turned me loose on the mountain.

After a couple of hours at the base pushing empty down-coming gondola cabins around the bull wheel to be loaded with skiers,

I was told to go to the bottom of the Prospector chair to relieve the operators for lunch.

I soon discovered two facts about loading skiers onto fast-moving chairs. First, the chair tries to tear your arm from its shoulder socket as you hold it for the skiers; and second, about half the skiers nearly poke your eyes out with their ski poles as they grab for the chair.

Often a skier would yell at me, "My partner's a first timer. Could you slow the lift?"

"Sure. You got it."

I didn't mind a charade if it would give a beginning skier more confidence. I'd try to get the skiers into position before I slammed them with the rapidly moving chair.

I was not always successful in this endeavor; in fact, I set some sort of record that still stands to this day. A twisted, tangled pile of skiers was accumulating right off my loading ramp. I marveled that people continued to do the quick sidestep to get into position for the next chair that would send them smashing into that heap of twisted humanity, but if that was what they wanted, I was there to oblige them.

After about 20 minutes of this, I began to work up a sweat. Taking off my coat, I hung it to the cord that ran overhead. Suddenly the lift came to a bouncing halt. Thank God – I could use a break. Besides, it gave the piled-up skiers a chance to get untangled. Most of them just skied to the end of the line, laughing. Several, for some reason, just stood there glaring at me. But in a moment I'd forgotten them as I poured a cup of hot thermos coffee.

Soon the crowd started to ask why the lift had stopped. All I could do was shrug.

"Beats me. Problems at the top of the lift, I guess."

All this time I could hear the phone ringing in the lift shack, but I was not about to desert my station to go and answer it.

Finally, sensing that this mob of skiers might turn ugly, I decided to answer the phone. The real reason was so that I could lock myself in the lift shack if they started to riot.

Barney Hyde, the operator at the top, wanted to know the nature of my problem. I informed him that I had no problem. I hadn't stopped the lift. Hell, I didn't know how to stop the lift if I wanted to. Barney gave me a crash course over the phone on how to operate the thing.

Taking my coat off the emergency-stop cord cleared the stop alarm and enabled the lift to start up. Soon I had the bell system down pat and, by shift end, had the job down pat too.

I was somewhat upset that the lift operators I'd relieved for lunch never did come back that day, but I soon learned that the attitude of some of the employees was "don't give a shit." Among them there was a feeling of betrayal and of being underpaid by the company.

The Treasure Mountains ski resort (now Park City Mountain Resort) had been built by the United Park City Mines Company with federal funds intended to revive depressed economies. Naturally, the employees who were the fodder that had ensured the granting of the loan thought they were at least entitled to a livable wage. By the time I started working for the resort, they had organized the Lift Operators' Union.

That first day at shift's end I traveled down the mountain in the gondola. As we passed through the angle station at mid-mountain, Ed Grose, the president of the union, slowed our cabin and handed me a union check-off form authorizing dues to be withheld.

"Sign it and return it to me tomorrow!" he shouted over the roar of the machinery.

I certainly didn't want to be branded a scab. Bad things happen to scabs in mining camps, and Park City was still a mining town. I joined.

Photo courtesy of the Kimball Archive.

It would be hard to find a more motley crew of union members. There were ex-miners; a few pensioners; a half-dozen small-business owners who were trying to subsidize their income until times got better; a roster of town drunks; a new breed that were known as hippies; and a few traditional ski bums. It's strange what will unite people in a common bond, but low wages, poor management, and cold feet seem to do the job.

Trapper Horan was the caretaker at the Summit House. In the winter, Trapper helped to unload the gondola cabins of skiers, telling them, "Pick up your skis and exit, please." He treated all skiers equally.

Once, when the great French skier Jean-Claude Killy was on the mountain competing on the racing circuit, he climbed from the gondola cabin, giving grace to all those present but not heeding Trapper's words. His skis made the 45-minute round trip down the mountain and back again on the cabin's ski rack. Needless to say, Killy was upset.

Trapper only shrugged. "He's no better than any other skier and not near as bright."

Then there was Frank Stint. About once a month or so, every time his wife phoned and told him that his paycheck wasn't in the mail, he'd try to call a wildcat strike. Usually he was unsuccessful.

Frank was one of the old-time operators who actually liked skiing. But he had a hard time keeping his feet close together, so he took to tying his ankles together. Though there was method to his madness, it never caught on with other skiers.

Bernard "Chink" Sessions was a rough old miner who worked at the resort for years. Damn, he had keen eyesight. Twice that I know of his eagle eyes saved the hide of a few employees.

The first was during summer maintenance when the gondola wouldn't start with remote control at the bottom of the mountain. Ed Grose went to the angle station and bypassed the safety switches to start it, with a warning to Chink and other employees riding in the gondola cabin to keep a sharp eye out for problems.

While sitting in the cabin as it approached the first ridge, Chink spied that the cable on Tower 14 had come off the pulleys and was running on top of the crossarm. The gondola cabin would soon smash into the tower! Tower 14 was the tallest on the mountain, over 100 feet high; the occupants' chance for survival was slim.

Chink didn't hesitate. As soon as he saw the danger, he flung open the gondola door and jumped. Fortunately, on the first ridge the cabin was only about 10 feet off the ground. He ran back over the ridge, waving his arms to catch the attention of the bottom operator, who shut down the lift. The gondola cabin stopped about five feet short of hitting the tower. Those other employees trapped in the cabin spent the rest of the day fidgeting while management figured out a way to get them down.

On another occasion I was with a work party going up on the gondola. As we approached the old Silver King Mine tailing dump, Chink studied the dump for a short while, then announced, "We're going to hit that damn pile!" Over the weekend a trail grooming crew had piled up a huge mound of rocks and soil right under the gondola path.

The rest of us in the cabin told Chink he was crazy – no one in their right mind would make a pile so high that a gondola cabin would hit it. But finally Ed Grose said, "By God, you're right. We're going to hit it!"

There were four of us in the cabin. Ed opened the door and positioned himself in the doorway, studying the ground. About halfway up the tailing dump the jump wasn't too bad – about eight feet. As soon as Ed had jumped, Chink bailed out after him. Don Neil got into position but just couldn't muster the courage to jump.

Five seconds later it was too late. We hit the pile of rocks and it all but turned the cabin over as the front windshield dragged through the pile. If the window had given way, the cabin would have become a large scoop shovel and we could have been crushed or suffocated.

Fortunately, with less weight in the cabin, the windshield held. The only misfortune was that Don Neil got his hands pinched black and blue when the cabin door slammed shut on them.

It was a great ride. Hell, they could have charge admission for it.

But the most thrilling ride I ever had on the mountain was when the foreman, Victor Buck, and I were spray-painting towers off the platform work car on the gondola lift. I was strapped in a boatswain chair and dangling 20 feet below the work car. Victor was communicating with the operator at the angle station by radio – or rather, he was trying to communicate.

The conversation ran something on the order of: "Base, do you read me? Move us uphill three feet. Over."

"Vic, is that you? I can't hear a damn thing! Please repeat."

Victor would repeat his message over again, and get the same reply.

After about twenty minutes of this, the operator said, "To hell with it. I'm going to bring you in so you can change batteries."

Victor yelled at me to get back to the work platform fast. He didn't need to. I was cranking with all my might. Victor pulled up the spray gun, and I was beginning to think that I would make it.

Then the lift started.

The surplus cable for the boatswain chair lay tangled on the ground below. As it was pulled through the brush along the ground, it would get caught. Whenever it broke loose, the boatswain chair – and I – swung a swing that Tarzan would have envied.

After the third great swing, I decided to take my chances on the ground. I kicked loose and did a near free-fall to the ground. I landed running because I was still strapped into the safety belt. Trying to undo a contraption like that while running in a bow-legged fashion is something I hope I will never be faced with again.

Somehow I managed to free myself. I was so happy to be in one piece that I couldn't be mad at anyone. Victor, though, chewed out the angle-station crew for close to an hour.

Skiers ride the J-bar lift at the base of Treasure Mountains, now Park City Mountain Resort.
Photo courtesy of the Park City Mountain Resort Collection, Park City Museum.

In 1968, the company promoted Ed Grose to assistant foreman. With one sweep of a double-edged sword, the resort had gained a competent administrator and stifled the union by removing its head. (No so-called "company man" – that is, anyone in management – can belong to a union.) In all likelihood, the company hoped that, without a head, the union would wither and die.

Almost immediately, several members of the union started to lobby for the job. Rumors, gossip and backbiting ran rampant.

To this day I'm not sure what took place at the next meeting, but when it was over I was astonished to find myself president. It was a dubious honor at best. Did they elect me for my leadership abilities or as a scapegoat in case matters went to hell?

After a few months I began to find my wings. I never learned to soar like an eagle, but more like a sparrow. I could squawk and peck and, at times, coo, if it would help sign up new employees into the union. I found myself buying more than my share of beer at the Rusty Nail bar. Anything to keep the rank and file happy.

Our contract with the resort provided good vacation and insurance benefits, grievance procedures and job protection. But the wages were low and there were no ski privileges. Most of the new employees thought that skiing was important, while the old hands would say, "Give me a decent paycheck and I'll buy my own damn ticket if I want to ski."

As time went on, it became more apparent that conditions wouldn't improve unless we could bargain from strength. Our parent union was the Building and Construction Trades Union. I decided that we could do better with the United Steelworkers Union, which had represented Park City miners for many years, and we had a common foe, United Park City Mines, owner of the resort.

My simple solution, though, turned out not to be so simple. The mine company fought us every step of the way.

The day of the election I was a nervous wreck, as though I myself were on trial. Being a poll-watcher was a strange experience. Neither side could speak of the ongoing election because of the rule of silence, and making small talk with "company men" was somewhat akin to having teeth extracted.

Finally, all votes except one were cast. The last to vote was the son of the superintendent of the mining company. He'd been injured skiing earlier that day, and they brought him in to the poll on a stretcher. It was a gallant, but futile, effort on the part of the company.

We won! There were only two votes against the new union. Clem Hanson, president of the mining union, would now be in charge. Funny, I went from president to job steward and was happy about it. Both jobs paid the same – nothing.

The struggle was all uphill. We had our share of bitter contract negotiation, but we had fun too.

I will admit to a little malice on our part. A skier had written a letter praising the kindness and help she'd received on the First Time lift, the lift I operated. After Ed Grose read the letter on the bulletin board, he good-naturedly accused me of writing it myself.

That planted a seed in my mind.

There was an ex-surgical nurse working as a lift attendant on the First Time lift who, with my encouragement, developed a real knack for composing the grandest letters – praising the lift employees and taking an occasional shot at the rest of the operation. She'd use different stationery and alter her handwriting; then she would get ski tourists to mail the letters to the resort from all around the country. Office personnel posted many of the letters on the bulletin board, much to the embarrassment of management.

However, in 1971 the second shoe fell when Royal Street Corporation bought the resort from the mine company. The link we had formed with the mining union was now nullified. We were back to square one, and that's where we remained.

But in the long run labor was bound to fail at organizing ski resorts. The very nature of skiing and those who seek its employment defeated our attempt to keep a union in place. College dropouts waiting for the draft; hippies living from one party to the next; ski bums looking for the deep powder – they all had one goal in common: a good time. And that didn't include getting mixed up in a labor dispute.

Park City itself was changing rapidly. Families had been leaving town since the early 1950s, but now most left with remorse, and tears were common. People felt they had become strangers in their own home. Though few newcomers mourned their leaving, the quality of life dimmed with each departure. And with each new ski season there were fewer of the old-time lift operators. I loaded my last chair of skiers in the spring of 1973 and found employment elsewhere.

But I don't believe any of the old union lift operators felt that we failed. Like Don Quixote jousting with windmills, the battle had its own rewards. The many friendships formed during our brief struggle created a bond that stretches across the years.

Mike's Café

A tax assessor's photo of the Grover Café (left), 501 Main Street. In the late 1940s and early 1950s this building was the home of Mike's Café.
PCHS tax photo courtesy of the Park City Museum.

Mike Spanos probably couldn't have made a good living in the restaurant business even in more favorable times. Fortunately for him I doubt if the idea ever crossed his mind.

Mike's Café catered to the late-night trade: miners coming off night shift and those on day shift who had closed the bars and still didn't want to go home. It was a happy place, and maybe a lonely place, to be.

Many were "tramp" miners who would spend several months in Park City, then move on to another mining camp. Maybe they were leftovers from the Depression who got used to moving about and were never able to form roots again.

Mike was civic-minded and a great booster of Park City. He often helped organize the Fourth of July and Labor Day celebrations. I have heard it said he was instrumental in getting the ornate metal light posts on Main Street. And only Mike knows how many tramp miners he fed and, at times, boarded until they found work.

In the early 1950s gambling and liquor are what the public demanded and Mike, being public-minded, gave in to those demands. He maintained a classic back room in his café for his gaming customers.

There was also a room in the attic that was used for private – and I presume high-stakes – poker games. It could only be reached from an outside staircase in the back of the building.

Mike's Café, 501 Main Street, was dingy and somewhat dilapidated. A new layer of green paint would be added from time to time to cover the grime. (Before the building was demolished, I bought Mike's old roll-top desk. I had to remove six layers of green paint to find the natural oak.)

I didn't go into Mike's Café often. It did not cater to teenagers, though occasionally after a dance we would stop in for a sandwich. The coffee was the strongest I ever drank. It was made in one of those giant stainless-steel tank-like machines that, thank God, are seldom in use today.

But the food was good, and at times Mike would throw in extras. He had a favorite brand of pickled pepper and would travel from booth to booth urging his customers to try them, He swore, and I mean swore, that they were not too hot, and then demonstrated the proper way to eat them. Damn, I wish I'd had the guts to try one.

We were welcome there until we ventured into the back room to watch the action. After ten or twenty minutes Mike would run us out.

Those patrons of Mike's are now foggy in my mind. I do recall a few. There was Rudy Valla, a two-time loser who shortly thereafter would commit his third offense: robbing a liquor store in Norfolk, Virginia. He had dark, wavy hair, long sideburns, a spare cigarette perched over his ear, tattoos, sleepy eyes. And oh, how he loved playing the pinball machines!

I still remember him talking to the balls as they bounced from pin to pin. When finally one would come to rest in the right hole, he would exclaim, "That's a little dandy!"

Then there was Chuck Thomas, the marshal. He occupied the stool nearest the door, where he had a good view of the happenings on Main Street, and quaffed a vast quantity of coffee. About nine o'clock each night he would leave the café and make the rounds on Main Street, trying each door of the closed shops. The sound of his rattling each door would carry for blocks. He chose that time of night to make his rounds so he would not have to witness any wrongdoings at Mike's as the action picked up.

Mike Spanos stood about five foot seven and his frame was frail. His usual dress was a blue suit without a tie and an open vest; the seat of his pants was shiny from constant wear. He chain-smoked Prince Albert tobacco; he rolled his own cigarettes with speed and deft ability. Cigarette ashes often clung to his suit and vest.

Mike's Greek accent was heavy but easy to understand. He punctuated every utterance with gestures of his hands.

Before opening his café, Mike was in partnership with Mike Safianides in the Park Tavern. During Prohibition they ran a still that was hidden at Martin's Tunnel in Thaynes Canyon. I can't imagine what kind of bourbon they made – two Greeks whose taste buds were seasoned by ouzo. That may help explain why Wyoming whiskey was so popular in Park City.

Prohibition must have been good to Mike. He loved to talk about it, and could tell tales that made him laugh so hard he would go into a coughing frenzy that nearly put him on his knees.

The story I liked best was about a couple of his patrons that Marshal Tommy St. Jeor picked up for public intoxication. They were thrown into the dungeon in the basement of the old City Hall (now part of the museum).

One of those cells had a window, since bricked in, that was barred with heavy steel strapping in a gridiron pattern so tight that it was nearly impossible to pass anything to the prisoners within. Yet Mike managed to keep his friends drunk for their entire stay, much to the consternation of Marshal St. Jeor.

Mike said he took a roll of wax paper, spiraled it out into a long funnel and poured his illicit booze into the waiting tin cups below. At last he had a captive market for his hooch.

The building occupied by Mike's Café, on the northwest corner of Main and 5th Street (Trapper's Way), had once housed the popular Grover Café, operated by a Chinese man with the Americanized name of Joe Grover.

In the nineteenth century the Park City Chinese community was held in utter contempt by the genteel whites. But in time those feelings mellowed as the last Chinese citizens left for greener pastures. Finally only Joe Grover's son, Joe Jr., remained.

Grover had managed to corner the real-estate market in the dying camp, and was held in bondage by it. There was not a buyer to be found, even at giveaway prices. Joe Jr. was Mike Spanos's landlord.

There is one fun mystery related to this building. Many years ago, when the Paull Brothers and Wilson general store that abutted the café to the north was being torn down, it was discovered that the store had somehow tapped into the café's hot-water system. There is no one alive who can explain this mystery.

It's hard to conceive of Tom Paull or Archie Wilson having the ability or personality to do such a dastardly deed. I have tried to imagine them in a daring dead-of-night raid on the restaurant next door, spectacles on their noses, plumbing tools in hand, a lantern turned low.

No, I guess the mystery will remain.

In the fall of 1954 Mike Spanos decided to enlarge his operation and include girls. He moved from his old café to the Salt Lake House on the other side of Main Street.

The Salt Lake House, 418 Main Street, was a grand hotel in its day. It was a two-story frame building that had the most unusual front façade. White wood shakes were used in a staggered manner to form a kind of crescent design. It was trimmed in dark green.

However, the north wall had been exposed to the elements and was bare of paint. The roof line had begun to sag and the walls had a slight bulge. The gigantic icicles that formed on the building during the winter did much to explain its sad shape.

Prior to Mike taking it over, the building had been used as a rooming house and had served as a refuge for many old-timers and a few winos. Many of the rooms had Hercules powder (dynamite) boxes nailed outside the windows; they served as excellent iceboxes for most of the year.

The only occasion that took me into a tenant's room is a story I do not relish telling.

Our gang was on its way to a dance at the Vets' Hall (the old Washington School). As we swaggered down Main Street we bumped into the father of one of our key members. He, being a little tipsy, decided to treat us to a small social drink. He motioned for us to follow him into the Salt Lake House. We filed up the rickety staircase and down the dimly-lit corridor until he stopped at a door, reached up to the transom and retrieved a skeleton key. "This is Tony Baloney's room," he said, pulling a gallon of wine from under the bed, "but the jug is half mine. It's the best damn Dago red you'll ever taste."

The Salt Lake House as it looked in the winter of 1947-48.
In 1954 Mike Spanos moved his café into this building.
Photo courtesy of the Kendall Webb Collection, Park City Museum.

After each of us had a liberal libation, we made our way to the Vets' Hall to dance to the music of the Bircumshaw orchestra.

The music was right out of the 1920s. It had a jerky, bumping rhythm we found impossible to dance to. The Bircumshaw band had not played in public for years and I thought it showed. But the older people there seemed to love it and the floor was crowded with dancers.

Anyway, during the course of the evening several of our gang disappeared from the Vets' Hall. It dawned on me that they had gone back for another drink of wine. Grabbing my friend Little Joe, we made a dash for the Salt Lake House. We weren't going to let them get that jug without us.

On creeping down the dark corridor, we had second thoughts. What if they weren't there, or if we were caught? Tony Baloney – his real name, I think, was Balachi – had kind of a wild-man reputation with us kids. For years he had lived under the China Bridge, and for years we had tossed rocks from the bridge onto his roof. Watching him charge out of his cabin, cussing and waving his arms in frustration, was great sport. There was no way he could catch us. But tonight he might.

Tony stood about five foot six and was stooped with age. He had a full snow-white handlebar mustache stained bronze in the center from chewing Horse Shoe plug tobacco. It was his room, but if our friends were in there we would never live it down.

The door was ajar, and the room was lit by a dim, low-wattage bulb that hung from the ceiling. The room was empty.

Well, we just had to check to make sure that no one had absconded with that jug of wine.

Now, I don't know what Tony Baloney thought when he walked into his room and found two juvenile punks sitting on his bed, sipping his wine. He didn't say a thing as he walked past us and went to the closet. But when he spun around holding the longest butcher knife that I have ever seen, I suddenly knew the meaning of the old saying, "Actions speak louder than words."

Joe and I climbed over each other trying to reach the door, the corridor, the staircase, the lobby, the street, not daring to look back.

It was an episode I'm not proud of. My only defense is that it was the best damn Dago red I ever tasted.

When Mike took over the Salt Lake House, he did some remodeling. He located his restaurant in the south end of the building, where the office of the miners' union, Local 4264, had been. It was smaller than the old café, but everything was new and shiny. Mike hung a large red sign with lettering traced in neon. It was the first remodeling or new construction on Main Street in a long, long time. People were proud.

The back room was directly east of the kitchen, but I never had the privilege of being admitted. The girls were upstairs, through the old lobby on the north.

The door at the top of the staircase was now locked, but there was a buzzer and nearby a hand-penned note tacked on the wall reading, "Ring for Service." And ring we did.

Some nights when we were bored we would hang out on the street in front of the Salt Lake House. Invariably our talk would turn to the second floor of Mike's, and then to whom had enough guts to go and ring the bell. Invariably one of our number would be shamed into creeping up those stairs and ringing the buzzer. Then we would run like hell!

Mike's proprietorship of the Salt Lake House was short-lived. On a Saturday night, the 16th of April, 1955, he was caught up in the big raid along with the proprietors of several other Park City back-room operations.

Earlier that night my friends and I had been run out of the Park Tavern by the night cop, so we took up residency in The Oak, across the street from the Salt Lake House, and were shooting pool when the raid began.

Sirens, flashing lights, flashbulbs, deputies running all over the place, reporters and photographers tripping over themselves.

A *Deseret News* reporter wrote that the raiders "struck with the speed of vigilantes" and that's exactly how Park City felt about the raid. We saw the officers as an unlawful mob using extra-legal means with no constitutional authority to loot Park City of its heritage.

It was an exciting night. We watched and hooted, "There goes Park City's tourist trade!" as the vigilantes led two handcuffed, frightened girls to a waiting car.

Mike was arrested and charged with keeping a house of ill repute, gambling, and selling liquor illegally. His bail was set at

$900. I still remember the pompous, smug look on the deputy's face as he placed the hasp and padlock on Mike's Café.

Mike posted bail and pretty well beat the charges against them. After all, an innkeeper rents rooms. What his tenants do was not his concern. They say that when the judge asked Mike if he was keeping a house of ill-fame, he replied, "I don't keep Elaine, or any other girls. Besides, I pay Social Security on all employees. What you want from me?"

I think the judge became as confused as Mike appeared to be.

No one was gambling that night, and cards, chips and other paraphernalia do not constitute a crime. As for liquor, a man is entitled to have a little on hand for his own indulgence.

But Mike's fight was gone, his spirit was broken, and his health was poor. The fun had been taken out of the game. The time had come to let the state win.

In reading some old correspondence from the desk Mike once used, I found he was not much different from any other small businessman. He was fending off bill collectors while trying to collect money owed him.

One letter in the desk was written by an inmate in the Colorado State Penitentiary. He asked Mike to check a rumor that the mines were going to pay the back wages due to many miners. And he promised he'd settle up his account with Mike if he would help him collect his back pay.

The last paragraph read something like, "I guess you're wondering why I'm writing from here. It kinda seems like this store kinda got robbed. And they kinda found me there, and I kinda had this gun, and they kinda thought that I kinda had something to do with it."

It kinda goes like that at times.

Years later the Kiwanis Club was raising money by demolishing old buildings in Park City. As I member of the club I helped with many of these projects, but when it came to the Salt Lake House in August 1969, I balked. It was no big protest. I just didn't show up.

I reasoned that the structure had historical significance, and the façade had architectural merit. In reality I knew that there was a frail, white-mustachioed ghost with a long knife waiting for me.

A Walk up Main Street

Upper Main Street as it looked in the 1950s. Among the buildings visible on the east side of the street are the Utah Power and Light office, 506 Main, the Post Office, 450 Main, and the City Cash Market, 446 Main. *Photo courtesy of the Kendall Webb Collection, Park City Museum.*

Most of my stories take place at night, but I offer a sketch of Park City's Main Street, and the people who lived and worked there, to show that there was life before the sun set. A walk up Main Street on an early summer morning was always a delight.

On the lower east side of the street you could see Clara Mawhinney, hose in hand, washing the long boardwalk that ran from Main Street to the rear entrance of her boardinghouse at 136 Heber Avenue. She was a favorite of every kid in town, and was "Aunt Clara" to many. Though she detested cats, she accepted every stray that some neighborhood kid would bring to her for shelter.

Next, going up the east side of Main Street, would be Charlie Himes, who swamped The Cozy (596 Main) and swept the sidewalk in front of the establishment. Charlie also opened The Cozy for early trade, and during foul weather this meant providing a place of refuge for some of the town derelicts.

Next door you would see Mrs. McPhie in her housecoat, peeping out the broad plate windows of her storefront home. The structure had once housed her deceased husband's cigar factory.

Across the way the Prompt Cleaners (591 Main) had not yet opened. Cliff Roach was still up the street, swamping out The Oak tavern for his father Cappy.

Archer's Mortuary (586 Main), like all mortuaries, was surrounded by a pall. There was a viewing that day, so the doors to the parlor were left open overnight so early morning callers could pay their respects.

The first real job I ever had was at Archer's. Fortunately for me, it was also the only job my mother made me quit. I was disappointed. In three whole days of employment not one person died.

Across the street, working in her flower garden, was the widow Haufstein. Her garden would rival any in the state. She was a quiet, soft-spoken German national.

Years later, when I was running a grocery store – the first grocery store in town with a beer license – Mrs. Haufstein on occasion would purchase a single bottle of beer. She always explained that it was for beer soup, something she dearly missed for years, until I opened my store. (She was a lady and would not enter a tavern.)

Being curious, I got the recipe for her soup and tried it. You take one cup of beer, heat it not quite to a boil, then add one cup of cream, one tablespoon of sugar, and a quarter teaspoon each of cinnamon, ginger and nutmeg. Then serve piping hot.

Yuck! All I can say is the Germans have strange taste buds.

Next up the street was the New Park Hotel (573 Main). Herman Hethke could be seen watering potted plants in the lobby. It would soon be closed and boarded up, and its porch would become a favorite hangout for derelicts and winos.

Across the street the Lewis Brothers Stage just pulled out of its garage (570 Main). Virgil Bair delighted in honking and waving at everybody in sight. The bus took commuters to their jobs in Salt Lake.

The storefront Shepherd residence (562 Main), with its yellowing curtains, looked abandoned, but behind the building Mr. Shepherd was busy feeding his rabbits with a commercial rabbit food. The rabbit-food company also furnished Mr. Shepherd with cellophane-faced boxes to display the butchered product in its best possible light. His rabbits were a real bargain at sixty cents apiece. They were the best domestic rabbits that I've ever eaten.

The next building up on the east side was Tom Steward's barbershop (556 Main), still closed. It would be hours until he opened.

Next door, the Elks' Hall (550 Main) looked gloomy. It was hard to imagine but, after their regular meeting last night, the poker game didn't break up until three o'clock in the morning.

Clem Hansen was just opening the door to the Masonic Uinta Lodge 7 (530 Main). He was killing time while his wife was at a library board meeting. Then they would be off to Salt Lake to do some shopping.

Across the street, Pete Durante sat in the doorway of his Main Furniture and Hardware store (551 Main), soaking up the sun. A practice his son, Art, would have loved, if given the time.

The next building on the west side (541 Main) was vacant on the ground floor. It would be a year or so until Nola Baker opened her beauty parlor there. However, the second story had been a beehive of activity since 4:30 a.m. Every morning, Betty Jennings would roust her daughter Freddie and son Jim to get them on their way. The Salt Lake Tribune newspaper had to be delivered.

Next up the street, Jim Polychronis was supervising his son unloading a Jimmy (GMC) pickup truck of fresh vegetables. Jim's

Shown here in 1957, Pete Durante's Main Furniture and Hardware sold more than just furniture and hardware.
Photo courtesy of the Kendall Webb Collection, Park City Museum.

Palace Grocery (537 Main) had the reputation of carrying the best vegetables in the camp.

Across the street, the City Hall (528 Main) was coming alive. Judge Eddie Evans already had his second-story window open and was following his custom of gazing out on the street. He looked agitated as the downstairs police-station phone rang and rang.

In fact, all up and down the street, and even on lower Park Avenue, the police phone was ringing. On every block or so of Main Street, and less frequently on Park Avenue, there were cast-iron phone boxes on the east side of the street. As kids we soon discovered that a hard pull would pop open the locked doors of the police phone boxes.

Alas, with the old telephone-operator system, it was impossible to abuse them. The local operators knew all our voices, along with the voices of most everyone in town, and would not place calls for us on these phones. In fact, it was a fast way to get into trouble.

The phone soon stopped ringing. Undoubtedly the operator had located the marshal at lower Pop Jenks Café, having his morning coffee.

Lawrence Berry, the retired fire chief, was already next door at the fire station, checking the fire engine to make sure nothing had happened to it since he checked it late yesterday afternoon.

Mrs. Frieda Consoni was fumbling with keys, trying to open the library (518 Main) for an early library-board meeting.

On the west side of the street, the Taylor Building (523 Main) appeared to be vacant. It would be several months before Kendall

This Main Street storefront housed the Park City Library until 1982.
It is now part of the Park City Museum.
Photo courtesy of the Edgar Stern Collection, Park City Museum.

Webb moved into this new location. No one suspected that its second floor was being used as a teenager gang clubhouse.

Next door, Waldo Thompson, proprietor of Star Meat and Grocery (515 Main), wondered if he could get the old ice plant to run once more. Labor Day – and a demand for ice – was coming.

It would be an hour or so before Doc Sheen opened his dental office (513 Main) south of Star Meat and Grocery. Next to his office, the sheriff's office (509 Main), was never open.

Across the street, Ken Ryan (510 Main) came dashing out of his house, lunch bucket in hand, to catch the green New Park Mines employee bus parked in front of the Post Office. He didn't need to run. Caleb Cullen, the driver, would have waited for him.

The Utah Power & Light office (506 Main) had not yet opened for business, but the window displays were always worth viewing. This one was of arts and crafts by the Girl Scouts. Across the street, Mike Spanos studied the New Park Mine bus from the doorway of his café (501 Main), perhaps wondering how he could entice the miners into his breakfast trade.

The town marshal's first duty each day was to unlock the doors of the Post Office (450 Main). Most everyone in town stopped there at least once each day, some of us three or four times a day. There was always someone to visit with there.

Mr. Meeks, an old insurance debit man from Logan, would literally set up office there when he was in town. Half his clients whose premiums were due were bound to check their mailboxes that day and find Meeks, receipt book in one hand, the other hand stretched out. You didn't know if you should shake his hand or hand him money.

The Post Office grounds south of the building were like a well-kept park. The flowerbeds almost rivaled Mrs. Haufstein's for beauty.

One other thing the Post Office had, that no other business in town could boast of, was a decent sidewalk. No patches of black asphalt were holding the cement together. It did not heave up but was actually smooth, and there were hardly any cracks.

Across the street, Heine Hernon of The Club (449 Main) would not stir until 10:30 a.m. Then, like clockwork, he would stroll to the Post Office, then to Pop Jenks' for his standard breakfast: a short stack of pancakes and an egg, over easy, chased down by black coffee.

Next door, Mr. Tessman would not open his radio and small-appliance repair shop before noon.

The iron curtains on Art Piva's building (447 Main) would not open again under his proprietorship. He gave up the state liquor store franchise to try his luck elsewhere.

Across the way, Olga and John Aimo's City Cash Market (446 Main) was open for business. One could wonder why the word "Cash" was in the name of their market when they carried more than half the town's citizens on credit.

South of the City Cash Market, two buildings were vacant. Then came Oblad's 5 & 10 Cent Store (436 Main). Mrs. Florence Aubrey was in the back straightening up some merchandise.

There was a blue-enameled, mirrored penny scale that sat outside on the stoop next to the front door. It waited to tell the sidewalk pedestrians their weight and fortune. I believe that every kid in town knew that a hard jump on the scale would make the machine sputter out three or four tickets. But then the weight would not be stamped on any of the tickets and the fortunes could not be trusted.

On the west side of the street, George Keating, in faded navy dungarees, was hosing down the sidewalk in front of the Veterans' War Memorial Building (427 Main). He would time it to finish when the morning coffee crowd was departing Pop Jenks' for their respective jobs. Then he would take a leisurely coffee break. He loved to visit but did not like crowds.

George's job of managing the Memorial Building kept him going from early morning until late at night. He ran a taut ship and would not tolerate any horseplay from kids. But if you didn't abuse the system he was a great ally.

The Mountain States Telephone office (434 Main) was not yet open for business, but the door was left unlocked for the operators' shift change. The shades on the windows were still drawn. The massive sandstone windowsill was imbedded with iron spikes to prevent loiterers from sitting or leaning there. It gave the building a cold appearance.

Next door, Pop Jenks' Confectionery (430 Main) was the hub of the camp's morning activity. Nearly everyone who worked on

Wilma Larremore at the Mountain States Telephone switchboard, 434 Main.
Photo courtesy of the Wilma Larremore Collection, Park City Museum.

Main Street stopped in for breakfast or coffee. Pop (J.E. Jenkins) was kept busy in his kitchen, but every so often he would pop out to greet some seldom-seen customer, or help his waitress with some problem behind the counter.

Next up the street was the gutted, deserted *Park Record* building (424 Main). The Record was now being published in Morgan, Utah. The building would collapse before the coming winter was over.

Across the way, Les Taylor was late opening his barbershop. It sometimes happened after an Elks' meeting. Kendall Webb waited outside, hoping that Les would accept his new offer to buy the old Taylor Building (523 Main) down the street. Webb didn't suspect that Taylor was thinking about closing up shop and accepting a barbering job in Las Vegas, Nevada.

In front of The Oak saloon (415-419 Main), a group of old-timers were gathering to soak up the morning sun. In the afternoon they would cross over to the Salt Lake House and continue this ritual. Old Sol was always worshipped in Park City.

Pete Cunningham, dressed in a double-breasted dark suit with missing tie, was telling Swede (Albert) Carlson and Joe Street in his heavy Irish brogue that his little black dog was mad at him.

"It happens every time I go out on the town and have a wee bit too much to drink. Aye, that dog is worse than a wife. She will ignore me for two or three days, 'til she gets over it. An' by then I'll go out again."

Across the street, Dick Sawyer had already left his storefront home (410 Main) for his coal yard. Orders for Royal coal were finally beginning to come in. It was not that long until winter.

Next door, The Drift tavern (402 Main) was locked up tight; the business seldom opened before noon. But this day Doyle Mecham's new Cadillac was parked in front. He had evidently spent the night inside. His sister, Lavone Jones, was the proprietor of The Drift.

Across the way, Doc Gordon was just coming downstairs to unlock the door to his Central Drug store (411 Main). He didn't miss not having the morning coffee trade. He liked the quiet dignity of his establishment.

Russ Horan, manager of the First Security Bank (405 Main), was just finishing breakfast. He still had over an hour until he had to open the doors.

The door at Valley Studio (401 Main) was wide open. Kendall Webb had left his shop unattended and was still down the street, waiting for Les Taylor to show up.

Mrs. Hodgson had her old Cadillac parked illegally, on the wrong side of the street in front of her jewelry store (363 Main). She was waiting for the boy (Ray Sanchez) from Mawhinney Motor to pick it up to have it serviced.

On the east side, Frankel's clothing store (368 Main) had recently closed its doors for good. The building appeared dreary.

Across the way in front of her storefront home (359 Main), Mrs. Davich was chatting with Father Cullen. The priest was sitting in the front passenger seat of a car. The car was being driven by Don Putman, a young Jack Mormon who delighted in chauffeuring Father Cullen or, for that matter, anyone who owned a car but did not drive.

Mrs. Davich was excited. It looked as though her son George was going to study for the priesthood. She would spend much of the remaining morning phoning friends and watering her houseplants. Her home was a veritable greenhouse.

Nearby, John McAlevy stood on the sidewalk, studying the vacant lot (356 Main) where the American Theatre once stood. He had overseen the demolition of the building for Chick Lloyd. Chick had donated the lumber to help rebuild Johnny Fritch's garage, which had burned in a recent fire.

Standing next to John was young Johnny O'Neil, a mute lad of nine. He had taken to following John around, Perhaps John had become a father figure to the boy since his father, Con O'Neil, had died.

Up the street, Earl Reseigh had just opened the door to Earl's Market (350 Main). The first thing he did was check the alarm clocks that were on display. It was a habit he had acquired of late. It seemed that someone would set the alarms to go off at his busiest time of day.

The Egyptian Theatre (328 Main) would be locked up tight until 6:30 p.m. Then Chick Lloyd would unlock the doors and turn on the marquee lights. It was business as usual.

The Park Tavern (322 Main) usually opened around 10 in the morning. Before that you could find Mike Safianides, the proprietor, working in his vegetable garden just south of China Bridge. His zucchini squash was the best in town.

On the west side of the street, Helen Tippett was at her place behind the counter in Mike's clothing store. She hoped there would be some customers that day; it was lonely being in the building by herself.

The Utah State Job Service Office (309 Main), that everyone called "the Unemployment Office," had not yet opened. Already there were four or five men waiting in front of the door. Their good cheer and jesting seemed hollow.

Next door up the street, Mrs. Hazel Taylor was behind her desk at the Board of Education building (301 Main). Superintendent Carl Winters would not be in until that afternoon. As a Mormon bishop he was presiding over a funeral that morning at the Second Ward.

Across the street, the waiting room at Dr. Dan Oniki's office (310 Main) was filling up. He would be in as soon as he had finished his rounds at the Miners Hospital.

Next door, Joe Davich was opening the doors of The Grill (304 Main). He was only now becoming comfortable in his new role as proprietor. Since his father's death, many things were rapidly changing. He hated quitting school to keep the family business running. But being appointed to fill a vacancy on the city council was a real honor, and now that his younger brother was studying to be a priest, things were really looking up.

On the west side of the street, the "big store" (239 Main) was just opening. Fraser Buck had pangs of nostalgia as he turned the key to Welsh Driscoll & Buck's department store. He had come to the decision that the store would have to close its doors for good. Business had been off for a good while, creditors were beginning to hound him, and most accounts receivable were uncollectable.

Fraser had studied the standard contract of a professional liquidation company. Maybe in the autumn he would give them a call. Summer was just too nice.

Nearby, Joe Pezeley was standing outside the New Deal Market (204 Main). Joe's father, Si Pezeley, had named the establishment after President Franklin Roosevelt's New Deal policy. In fact, Si had once run for mayor on his New Deal Party ticket – but only when the Democratic candidate was, in Si's eyes, not Democratic enough.

Joe was talking to his uncle, John. They were worried about Si's health. But both John and Joe knew that Si would not listen to them.

Inside the store, Si was bellowing for Joe to come in and give him a hand. As Joe started for the door, John shrugged and started across the street, into the sun.

This is as far as I will take the reader on this walk. I realize there were many aspects of the street that I missed, but I hope the feel of a community comes through.

Foolin' with the Food Chain

Movies being filmed in and around Park City today are so common they hardly turn heads. But way back then that wasn't the case. Heads not only turned, but many a native made his acting debut and the promotion was a community affair.

The first movie filmed in Park City, "Rusty and the Falcon," was made in 1957 when I was in the Navy. Years later I saw it on television. It followed the lines of all young-boys-and-pets scripts: Pet wrongly accused of destruction. Mean neighbor plots the demise of pet. Through trials and tribulations, pet is vindicated in the end and everyone lives happily ever after.

It was fun seeing friends and neighbors on the screen. George Keating was superb as the villain, considering his only training for acting tough was managing the War Memorial Building and forcing the youths of the mining camp to toe the line while using its facilities. No Hollywood makeup artist could have duplicated the pug looks of Larry Bye, seen staring at the falcon from a tavern window. And, in the background, the old mining camp sparkled, unspoiled by the overbuilt monstrosities of this era.

When I worked for the ski resort in the 1960s, nearly all the lift operators would be laid off each spring. A handful of the senior operators would be offered summer jobs, but at first I did not fall into that category. I was desperate for work one spring when I learned of another movie to be filmed in Park City. I applied and got a job as a "grip".

Grip, hell! I became a jack-of-all-trades: truck driver, equipment handler, set builder, painter, assistant animal handler and all-around fetch-it man. The job paid minimum wage, but I made a remarkable discovery: Jobs could be fun.

For the most part, the people I worked for – and with – were great. They loved what they were doing and it was a communicable disease. For the first time in my life I would bound out of bed, wondering what weird and wonderful task I would be faced with that day.

It was Frank Zuniga's first chance to direct a movie. He had scouted several states, looking for just the right spot for his production when he discovered Park City. He bragged to his movie friends that it was the perfect spot for shooting "The Owl That Didn't Give a Hoot": virgin country, unspoiled and unknown by the cinematography lenses. The disappointment showed in his face when I told him that "Rusty and the Falcon" had been filmed there several years earlier.

In reality, "The Owl That Didn't Give a Hoot" was nothing more than a remake of "Rusty and the Falcon." But I didn't give a hoot. Nor did Walt Disney, who thought that bird flicks were great for his "Wonderful World of Color."

My first days were spent working on the outside set in Snyderville. They had rented an old farm and had me paint the woodshed, chicken coop and other outbuildings an off-color mud gray.

The strange thing was that all the outbuildings had recently been painted a bright white. Mike Lonzo, the assistant director and main cameraman, said the white paint didn't look "real". I knew then that this was a different type of job.

Among my duties, I became the only professional dart-thrower that I know of. In the room of the boy star (David Potter) was a dartboard.

"It's too new," Mike said. "It's got to have that used look." He assigned me the task of throwing darts for several days to give it that used look.

One scene had Dave and his pet owl exploring the creek in the canyon behind their farm. The scene called for the owl to be excited by seeing fish swim by. I spent an afternoon at Flinders' farm, where they had a commercial kids' fishing pond, wielding a butterfly net and wading around in waist-deep water, netting fish. Best yet, I was being paid for it.

The inside sets were located in the old Mormon First Ward chapel, now known as the Blue Church Condominiums. One morning my grip partner, Gib Martinez, and I worked hanging wallpaper in the set's living room. We were just finishing up when Mike came by and exclaimed, "My God, you've hung it upside down!"

He was really upset. Gib and I thought it looked fine. Everyone who came by was brought into the argument. It raged for several hours. Irvin Park, the still photographer who hardly ever voiced an opinion, said he thought it looked okay. The majority said it looked good ... in all likelihood just to rile Mike.

But we were ready to repaper the room – after all, we were paid by the hour – when Frank came in and sided with Gib and me. Thereafter, every time Mike entered the set he looked at the wallpaper and shook his head in disgust.

I laid carpet on a staircase that went nowhere. "It's too new; it's got to have a worn look," Mike said. I spent several hours with a belt sander giving it that worn look.

⚒ ⚒ ⚒

The one job I hated was cleaning up after the owls. They had 16 for this movie and, God, could they make a mess. The stench would permeate whatever space they occupied. I guess a diet of beef hearts and mice will do that. I've read that owls can't smell; damn, they're lucky!

The owls would eat about 200 white mice or kangaroo mice a week, which we kept in a garage in Snyderville. On hot summer days the stench would become so intense that I hated entering the structure.

One of the owls had an independent mind and flew the coop. After a week or so, when Dennis Grisco, the bird trainer, was about to give up hope, it paid a surprise visit. Excitedly, Dennis yelled at me to get him a mouse.

I ran to the garage, forgetting to fill my lungs with fresh air before entering. Blinded by the lack of sunlight, I stumbled around, groping for the galvanized garbage can that housed the mice. I found the can and felt through the urine-soaked sawdust until I caught a mouse.

Gagging, I burst through the door, holding the mouse in triumph at arm's length. Suddenly, I saw the shadow of wings and heard a whooshing sound as the wayward owl ripped the mouse from my grip. That was as close as Dennis ever came to recovering the owl.

Years later, a friend of mine and his new bride rented the Snyderville property. They soon discovered the place was infested with white mice. Even after I explained the Hollywood connection and told his wife how envious the neighbors would be, she could see no honor in it. They moved out shortly afterwards.

The kangaroo mice deserved better than being on an owl's menu. They were cute and cuddly and had no fear of humans. I once suggested to my wife that I should smuggle some home and free them from their ultimate destiny. My wife, like the Snyderville bride, could see no honor in what I was suggesting.

One scene called for the owl to attack the kite that his master was flying. But owls don't attack kites. Finally, they fell on the idea of placing a mouse on top of the kite. The only problem was that the mouse kept peeping over the edge of the kite and stealing the scene. After three days of assembling and flying kites, they managed to find a mouse that was not a ham and kept out of sight.

There was also a difficult and potentially dangerous scene that called for the boy, the owl and a rattlesnake to be seen in the same frame. The boy was to be napping under a tree while his grand pet, perched in a tree, watched over his master. When a dastardly rattlesnake slides through the grass toward the boy, the owl, in the nick of time, spies the snake and flies to his master's defense.

Frank had ordered four huge, healthy and very expensive rattlesnakes from a reptile farm in California. He instructed us to make sure the snakes did not have any venom in their bite, just in case something went wrong and the snake got to the boy.

No one on the crew had any experience with rattlesnakes. However, we had seen snakes on public television being "milked". How hard could it be?

We stretched a piece of old inner tube over a quart canning jar and tried retrieving a rattler from the galvanized garbage can with hot-dog tongs. After 45 minutes of cursing, running, screaming and jumping, we had a snake. But try as we might, we couldn't get one drop of venom from it. In all likelihood the reptile farm had milked the snakes before shipping them. But there was no way to know for sure.

About then Frank announced they were set up for the shot and told us to bring the snake. Out of desperation, Gib produced a pair of pliers and said, "Give me the damn thing!" He extracted the fangs with medical precision.

The shot would have been okay if the owl had known his part. He was curious and did go for the snake. But instead of attacking it, he landed on its back, spread his wings and rode the snake. It was not very convincing.

After a conference, they decided to place four of the owls on a snake diet and ordered a batch of King snakes for that purpose.

In the meantime, we knew that the rattlers would be getting hungry, so we placed a couple of mice in the cage. But a strange thing happened. The mice got hungry first and started nibbling on the snakes. By the time we discovered this, so much damage had been done that one of the snakes died. To this day, I don't know if snakes are just plain dumb, or if the high altitude of Park City affected their metabolism.

Frank demanded that we remove the mice immediately. But it was much easier to put them in the cage than to extract them. It took us several hours.

The next shot with the rattlesnakes worked great. The owl associated snakes with food and went after the rattler with a ferocious appetite.

There was another complicated scene that called for the owl to crawl into a laundry hamper and somehow get dumped into the washing machine. They used a stuffed owl to swirl through the wash but wanted a wet, staggering owl to make a comic exit. But owls don't like water, and they never stagger.

They struck on the idea of getting the owl drunk. Frank produced a fifth of Chivas Regal Scotch whisky, and I gave the owl a demonstration of how it should be consumed.

After about two shots administered with an eye-dropper, and a dousing with a bucket of water, the owl got the scene right and, I believe, developed a taste for expensive Scotch.

At that time Park City had a huge flock of pigeons, and Mike wanted to film them from the top of the old Mormon church using a camera equipped with telephoto lenses. I was assigned the task of keeping the pigeons airborne. I raced around town in my old car, honking the horn, screaming and, when that didn't work, charging into their midst, shouting and throwing rocks.

Many a citizen watched me in wonder. One old native, shaking his head in disgust, muttered, "That's a Kimball for you. Oh, his poor mother."

A few years after this, Park City's pigeons disappeared. In all likelihood they caught some sort of virus. But I have one friend who's convinced that the hippies of that era ate them. I favor the theory that some of the more affluent restaurants, seeing a market for quail under glass ...

I hesitate to mention that this movie also documented my debut as an actor. The scene was set in a barber shop and I was getting a haircut. The owl flew into the shop and the startled barber, electric clippers in hand, cut a path from the base of my neck almost to the crown of my head.

I had been around the camera for months and being on screen didn't seem any different. That is, until the movie was to be shown. My whole family gathered around my mother's television set. At the last moment I remembered that I needed to do something at home and made my escape. I watched it alone, and still feel the cringe of embarrassment. Strange. I've gone through life making an ass of myself. Why should I object to it being captured on film?

I only got to see the movie that one time. Today I would pay dearly to have a copy of it. To be able to check on my recollection that neither the wallpaper nor the dartboard was ever shown. To be able to see old Park City as it once was.

I'm sure that the treatment of movie animals has vastly improved over the past 30 years. I hope so.

I realize that it was far from a great movie, but if it was good enough for Walt Disney, it's good enough for me.

Big Mountain

J.E. Jenkins (Pop Jenks) tickled the palates of Park City residents and visitors at two locations. One was the confectionery at 430 Main Street. The other was on the north end of town, near the intersection of State Route 224 and what is now Kearns Boulevard. He ran Pop Jenks Café from 1937 until shortly before the building burned in 1966. A favorite local hangout, the café had a back room with a dance floor, good music and food. Today (2022) the site is occupied by Squatters Roadhouse Grill. *Photo courtesy of the Pop Jenks Collection, Park City Museum.*

In the summer of 1959 I moved back to Park City after living in Salt Lake for nine months.

Back then I was given to little exaggerations, trying to impress my no-account friends. I boasted about all the women I knew in Salt Lake, giving the impression I was a man-about-town.

Most friends took my stories with a grain of salt, but two seemed to hang on every utterance. I swelled with my stories. Both friends were a couple of years older than me but their night-life was suffering badly.

Darrell was well liked, loved to laugh, could tell a good joke and had many male friends, but was shy around girls. "When I'm around girls," he'd laugh, "I just know they think I've been beaten by an ugly stick."

Nick, on the other hand, was somewhat of a social outcast. He had a sneering attitude and laughed at people, not with them. He had one redeeming quality: He owned a car.

Darrell suggested that I line them up with dates. Nick latched onto this idea and would not let it go. It became a taunt: "Line us up! Line us up!"

I had never fixed anyone up on a blind date and knew it was a bad idea. But it looked as if I might be caught in a bald lie if I didn't come through. I'd lose what little credibility I had.

There was a problem. I had exaggerated a little. The few girls I had met were from bar-hopping. I knew a few by name but didn't have one phone number. If I failed, Nick would never let me live it down.

Damn social misfits! I accepted their challenge.

After racking my brain, I could think of only one girl in the whole of Salt Lake that I knew well enough to phone. She was the younger sister of one of my best friends, Raymond. She had always been off limits when he was around. But this summer Raymond was working in the Uinta Mountains cutting timber, and there's an old saying that when the cat's away the mice will play.

Myrna was about three or four years younger than me but she was awful pretty. In my gut I knew it was a mistake, but what was I to do? My honor was at stake. I reached for the phone.

I convinced Myrna to go out with me and to line up my buddies with two of her friends. We picked up the girls the next evening about 6 p.m.

When Park City boys don't know what do to or where to go, they always head for Park City where they know where the action is.

By the time we reached Park City, enough information had been exchanged to know this would be a different evening. The age difference between Nick and Darrell and their dates was vast: 24 to 17!

Saloons and bars were out of the question. So reluctantly we went to lower Pop Jenks' Café where there was a backroom with a dance floor, good music and food.

I prayed that it would work out. It didn't.

In truth, Nick and Darrell had never been out with such cute girls in their lives. But that didn't matter. They did not want to be seen with what they termed jail bait. So they spent most of the time in the front of the café playing the pinball machine.

Even 17-year-old girls know when they are being ignored. Consequently, these two girls showered me with attention – an experience quite new to me and grand for my ego – though Myrna was doing a slow burn.

To cut a long story short, Darrell decided to stay in Park City. The trip back to Salt Lake was uneventful except that I discovered my standing with Myrna was zilch.

After a short good-bye, I learned that Nick wanted to stay at his brother's place in Salt Lake. He volunteered to drive me home, but through the tone of his voice I knew he was going to play up the great hardship it was causing him. I could visualize a long ride up the canyon listening to him whining.

I told him I too would stay in town – with my brother. I got out of his car on 2100 South at about 700 East and, as soon as he was out of sight, started hitchhiking. I probably could have stayed at my brother's place, but it was still early, and it was Saturday. I knew there was life in Park City. Hitchhiking and I were old friends. I figured I'd be home in a couple of hours.

I was picked up by a gay man. After a polite but firm rejection of his advances, I was dropped off at the mouth of Parley's Canyon where the old Stillman's Bridge stood on U.S. 40.

It was dark and traffic was slow. Slow? Hell, there was *no* traffic. I cussed Nick. I cussed Darrell. I cussed the girls. And I vowed never to fix up anyone on a blind date again!

Only five vehicles sped past me during the first hour. Then an old black '46 Mercury shot by me. I saw its brake lights come on as it swiveled to a stop a quarter mile up the road. I started to run toward the car as it backed up.

Five young men were in the car. It was obvious they were drinking. Laughing and hooting, they invited me to get in. Hell, this was okay – a party on wheels. I might salvage the evening after all.

As we sped up the highway, the kid seated next to me handed me a bottle of beer with the announcement that this was the last of the beer. The driver piped up that they still had an unopened case in the trunk of the car. He slowly coasted to a stop.

The driver and one of the front passengers got out. I could hear some cussing. The passenger stuck his head in the open window and announced, "Old bird-shit-for-brains lost the key to the trunk."

With that, the car emptied except for me and the one kid sitting next to me. Everyone was searching for the key. My new friend was pumping me for information on how I ended up hitchhiking, the events leading up to it, about Park City, and what have you.

About then a semi-truck passed us and, seeing we were in some sort of trouble, pulled off the road a little in front of us. By then the missing key had been found. I could hear one of my new companions call out, "Give me the tire iron. Give me the tire iron!" A cold chill traveled my spine. I could be in trouble.

The truck driver sensed something afoul and drove off. I did not want to believe I was in danger; often my imagination gets caught in high gear. To be on the safe side, I mentioned to my host that I had only a few dollars on me but I had unlimited credit in many of Park City's taverns. Moreover, I could line them up with girls pretty enough to die for.

Much to my dismay, they turned off U.S. 40 onto State Highway 65 and headed toward Little Mountain. Little Mountain was a popular place for lovers to park and there were several cars around its summit. Then the driver claimed he had taken the wrong road, turned around and headed toward Big Mountain. As I toyed with my beer bottle, a sick feeling entered the pit of my stomach. Damn, I wished I could control my imagination. I did not want to believe what was happening.

The kid seated to my left (I was between two in the backseat), sensing my fear, told me they were going to his dad's cabin to get some more beer. His father, he said, kept his horses there. He then went to some lengths to describe the horses.

I began to relax. I knew shit about horses but tended to trust horse people. Then I noticed a sign we were passing: "No Animals Allowed on the Watershed."

My heart sank. My brain was spinning, grasping for ideas. Oh God, what to do? All I could think to do was play dumb, the one thing I was good at.

Big Mountain was a major landmark on the old Mormon pioneer trail. State Highway 65 traversed towards its summit with a series of switchbacks. It was a narrow, winding road.

The car pulled to a stop at the top of Big Mountain. The talkative one said that we would have to walk to the cabin. I tried to beg off, saying that I had been walking most of the night and would wait for them in the car.

The driver, in a loud voice, said, "Out!" I gulped, fingering my now empty beer bottle, uttered a prayer, and slowly got out of the car.

The five of them formed a half-circle around me. The car was to my back. Due to the large amount of beer they had consumed, they were relieving themselves. The first one done asked, "Now?" A reply came in unison, "Not yet."

Without thinking, I picked out the smallest one and swung the beer bottle with all my might. On contact the bottle went flying out of my hand without breaking.

I did not stay to see my handiwork. I sprang over him, running across the highway and over the embankment. Falling, rolling, tumbling, I came to a stop – plumb in the middle of the highway on one of the switchbacks.

Getting to my feet in a limping run, I crossed the road and performed my tumbling act again. Before losing my footing, out of the corner of my eye I spied the headlights of their car coming around the corner. Again I picked myself up off a switchback, limped across the highway and tumbled off the edge.

This time, though, I moved more slowly, half walking, half sliding. I found a pine tree and slid under its heavy foliage. In the distance I could hear them searching, cussing, taunting, and threatening what they were going to do when they found me. "You're a dead man!" kept echoing in my ear. Their commotion was muffled by my thumping heart and screaming lungs.

They searched for me for what seemed like hours but probably was only minutes. At one time one of them passed within a few feet of my hiding place. It's surprising how long a person can hold his breath.

Even after they left, and I could hear their car moving down the road, I did not stir. It might be a trap. I could visualize a couple of them secluded, waiting for me to reveal my hiding place.

For over an hour I waited. It was pitch black, one of the darkest nights of the year. Slowly I crept out of my hiding place and slid down to the roadway. I was as quiet as could be, straining my eyes and listening for any sound. I found a fist-sized rock and hugged it for security. If I had to fight I would not lose this rock as I had the beer bottle!

Slowly I walked down the highway. Each road sign, I convinced myself, was a parked car, waiting. The sound of a deer moving off in the brush was terrifying.

As dawn approached and I could see farther, I became more confident and my stride lengthened. By the time I reached the junction with U.S. 40 (now I-80) my fear was replaced with rage.

It was only a short time before I caught a ride to the Sky Line garage and café at Parley's Summit. I ordered coffee, then phoned the Utah Highway Patrol and told Larry Rasmussen about my ordeal. Larry scolded me for hitchhiking but showed more compassion than the officer who showed up to interview me.

I came away from this experience a wiser man. And to this day I have never fixed up another person with a blind date.

Acknowledgements
Gary Kimball

There are so many who have helped me with these writings, it's hard to know where to begin. One problem is that these stories are scattered over my lifetime, but only committed to paper during the last decade or so. It is impossible to remember everyone and I'm sure the guilt will show.

I want to thank everyone who was or is connected with *Park City (Lodestar) Magazine,* especially David Hampshire, the first editor who showed both patience and kindness. He was followed by Kristen Rogers and Kristen Gould Case. Their tight editing, great encouragement and patience made many of my stories worth publishing. Don Weller's illustrations give movement and grace to some stiff characters. I also want to thank my brother Paul, who dug through his photo collection to find a few previously unpublished prints for me to use.

Gary Kimball, 2006

PART TWO

Growing Up in a Crumbling Town

A Kid's-Eye View of Park City before Skiing

Dedication

I would like to dedicate this book to all the friends and acquaintances I made while growing up in Park City, especially my high school class of 1955, the Double Nickel Class.

And to John E. Fritch, the best boss I ever worked for.

Gary Kimball

This Kendall Webb photo of the 7th grade boys in 1950 includes the author and many of his co-conspirators celebrated in this book. Five years later, many of them would graduate with the Park City High School Class of 1955.

Pictured here are:

Front row, left to right: David Colvin, Laurence Finnegan, Leo Sweatfield, Mont Goff, Jim Jennings, Fred Gillett and Bobby Berriochoa.

Second row: Jimmy Smith, Joe Richardson, Darrell Yates, Wayne Putman, Bob Mawhinney, Waldon Louder, Dean Hansen, Tony Kochevar and Roy Hamilton.

Third row: Clyde Maynard, Tom Daley, Pete Martinez, Donald Johnson, Arvil Price, Frank Provost, James Kinsey and Gary Kimball.

Photo courtesy of the Kimball Archive.

Preface to Part Two

Where and how to start a book has always been a problem for me. Part One, "Of Moths and Miners and Other Tales of Old Park City," was much easier. For the most part it was about landmark structures of the 1940s and '50s such as saloons and houses of ill repute, the people who operated them, and some of their customers. I also threw in a few less seasoned stories to give the book the semblance of balance.

Part Two is mostly about my memories as a boy growing up in a mining camp. At the time, the camp seemed to be teetering on its last legs. I decided to start with my earliest memories and work forward – just to show we were all born innocent.

Unfortunately, I have a tendency to jump from situation to situation, and back and forth in time, without telling the reader. But I presume that my readers are intelligent people who can follow my writing, and that there will be a few who will find it difficult to finish the book before telling me of my errors.

I hope this book will keep the reader engaged and maybe provoke an occasional laugh. Some stories might even elicit a tear or two. I admit it: I'm guilty of burying our heritage in nostalgia.

Of course, the main purpose in writing this is to give readers an idea of what Park City was before they discovered the place. I hope that their experience here is as rewarding as mine has been.

I have always believed that memories are similar to a diamond cut with many facets. When a group of people witnesses the same event, every person comes away with a different view reflecting their view of events, akin to the diamond's facets. Though different, all are valid.

Most natives consider "Old Park City" to be their Camelot. Though it's gone, our memories remain.

Gary Kimball, May 1, 2017

Born Innocent

A portrait of the author at the age of one.

I really don't know when my memories started. I have read where some people can actually remember being born, but I doubt these stories.

To me it seems the strongest memories people have are good memories. Being naked, wet, and spanked for no apparent reason would best be forgotten as soon as possible.

There is a picture of me as a one-year-old that I seem to remember being taken, but I'm sure I have that impression because my mother would carry me around the house as an infant and pause at that photograph and tell me about that day.

My first true memories were when I was four years old, early one summer evening, lying on the Ericksons' lawn with George Erickson, drinking buttermilk and "dubbing" stars. Each new star that appeared in the heavens one of us would dubs, and then we'd have a drink of buttermilk. (The Ericksons lived a little north of us across Woodside Avenue. George was a few years older than my father, and we were close neighbors and friends.)

It's a shame that I didn't do the same with my children when they were toddlers; maybe they would have few more fond memories to look back on, or at least a tolerance for a great drink.

The bombing of Pearl Harbor happened when I was four years old. I don't remember that day. I do remember Park City's and my family's involvement in the war, and by the time it ended, I was convinced that I had been a great help in winning it.

Sometime around the time America got pulled into the war, Dad traded in his old square-back Desoto. I got sick almost every time I rode in that car, probably because it had a faulty exhaust. One of those times came when we were going to Salt Lake. I could not remember the word "vomit" and didn't know any of the synonyms for the word. All I could say was, "I got ..." It soon became evident the word I was searching for.

Fortunately for me, Dad traded in that car for a 1937 Studebaker President. He was lucky to have purchased the Studebaker when he did. Because of the war, all kinds of restrictions applying to cars would soon be imposed. Gas and tire rationing became the rule of the day, and the speed limit was reduced to 25 mph.

I really loved that car. Its spare tire was placed in a recessed slot on the left side of the hood, just forward of the running board.

Running boards were great. In movies you would see car chases where the police would stand on the running boards to shoot at the fleeing bad guys. I couldn't wait until I had a chance to do that.

The car had a pretty paint job. They called it robin-egg blue. I don't know why, because it look green to me, but robin-egg blue *sounded* like a really neat color.

When the war started, Dad was working as a carpenter for the New Park Mine in Keetley, Utah. But he didn't think the job involved him enough in the war effort and he soon landed a job at the Dugway Proving Grounds in Utah's West Desert – building "Japanese" homes so the government could bomb them to determine the best method to destroy them. Unfortunately, that meant he had to stay and board there. He came home most weekends, but at times he would be away several weeks at a time.

When he came home I'd help him with his suitcase, knowing that he would usually bring me a treat – once a comic book, usually candy or gum. On one occasion I opened the suitcase and started searching for my treat. It's a shame my reading skills were poor at that age. I mistook some funny-shaped little pills for tiny-sized pieces of Chicklet gum – and soon discovered what a laxative was. My parents had a good laugh and I learned a lifelong lesson: Parents at times can be real cruel.

The war engulfed the whole nation; it even reached down to touch the youngest of us. One of the first things I recall was that there seemed to be a perpetual drive to sell war savings bonds.

Not that anyone my age could afford to buy a bond. But the government had that worked out too: war savings stamps! In school each Friday we were all but forced to buy a 10-cent stamp, then paste it into a book. (The books were kept in the teacher's desk.) When the book was full, it could be traded in for a bond.

I don't know of one kid who ever filled up a book. I'll bet the government ripped off millions of dollars in unredeemed saving stamps. Most likely, the books ended up in the trash sometime after the war ended. But the Buy Bonds campaign did give us a new saying: On parting, instead of saying good-bye, we'd all say, "Buy, buy bonds!"

I spent my first few school years at Marsac Elementary (now the home of City Hall), where the days were too long and recess too short. Back then I would run home for lunch; Mom always had it ready and on the table. This was standard for many of the grade-school students, although some who lived farther away would bring their lunches. Back then, as it is today, it was called "brown bagging."

I had one great problem with going home for lunch. Right after the 10-minute noon news on KSL radio, Erle Stanley Gardner's Perry Mason show would come on. It was a 20-minute serial mystery and would take five weekdays to complete a "case." Unfortunately, I always had to leave home at 12:25 p.m. and run like hell to get to class before the second bell rang. Most often I made it, but every day I was left hanging about what happened those last five minutes on Perry Mason.

Of course, each show started with a summary of the last show to bring new listeners up to date, which gave me comfort. But come Friday, when the case was finally resolved, I'd miss finding out who done it!

Some might find it sad that one of my fondest memories of elementary school was listening to the radio at noontime. But, in looking back at those days, radio was indeed important to me. It was magic and could take me to new and different worlds.

On Saturday morning I loved "Let's Pretend," sponsored by Cream of Wheat cereal. Its theme song went: "Cream of Wheat is good to eat, we eat it every day. We sing this song, it makes us strong, and it makes us shout 'hooray'. It's good for growing babies, and grown-ups too, to eat. For all the family's breakfast, you can't beat Cream of Wheat."

I'd run around the house singing the theme song and demanding Cream of Wheat, and occasionally actually getting it.

"Grand Central Station," an adult show with the New York railroad station as a backdrop, followed this show. Following that was "Hollywood Presents," an adaptation of a current movie that often used the movie's stars as the radio actors. They were all very dramatic, with the announcer setting the scene and tone of each show. I was really hooked on radio and could fill many pages describing the shows I loved.

I didn't miss much school due to sickness. If I said I was sick, Mom would keep me in bed all day long – a boring proposition if I was faking.

I do remember missing one day while I was in the second grade. The next day Mrs. Johnson, our teacher, sent me and Mickey Brooks, who also had been absent, to the office of the principal, Mr. Hubert.

It was my first visit; I was terrified. Older kids claimed that he kept a belt hanging on the wall, and that he used it on students who misbehaved. I was so scared that I didn't dare look up at the walls, but later, not wanting my friends to think I was a chicken, I told them that I had seen the belt hanging there.

The day before, all the students in my class had given urine specimens to check for diabetes or some such thing. The nurse was in Hubert's office; she gave us paper cups and told us to pee in them.

We got to the restroom and discussed what she had said. I just knew that no one would want a cup of pee! We must have misunderstood her. Maybe she wanted water, so we filled our paper cups with water and returned them to her.

The next day, Hubert came into our classroom and pulled out Mickey and me. He told us that there would be no more fooling around, that he wanted us to pee in a paper cup. We gave him what he wanted, but for the longest time I thought he was really crazy.

Kimball's Garage as it looked in the 1930s with the Silver King Coalition Building in the background and the family's Desoto parked in front.
The boy on the tricycle in the foreground is either Gib or Paul Kimball.
Photo courtesy of the Kimball Archive.

I was born during the Great Depression, a period that was tough on my family, especially my father, Gilbert J. Kimball Sr. In 1929 he and his brother Robert had gone into debt to build the Kimball Garage, a service station on the corner of Heber and Park avenues. For its time it was a grand affair. With cement and steel making it fireproof, it was considered state-of-the-art construction. It had room to store several dozen cars to cater to those who placed their automobiles in storage during the winter months.

The grand opening took place a month or so before "Black Tuesday," October 29, 1929, the day that ushered in the Great Depression.

They held onto the garage for a decade, but finally were forced to lock the doors and walk away. Dad was proud that he didn't take out bankruptcy, but pride was about all he escaped with.

My brothers were all born in the Miners Hospital, but due to financial conditions I was born at home, the same home that Dad was born in back in 1899. This gave me great pride, a sense of entitlement and, I thought, bragging rights. It was much better that being born in the Miners Hospital, although I soon discovered that home birth could cause you trouble if you bragged about it too much.

I was told that Dr. Goodwin had delivered me, and Mom said I was a big baby who weighed 12 pounds at birth. I told all my friends this "fact." None of them weighed more than seven pounds at birth, and some held me in envy.

Unfortunately, there was a neighborhood girl, Thelma Ann Reseigh, who was several years younger and a hell of a lot brighter than me. She seemed to get the best of me every time I matched wits with her. Her father owned Earl's Market at 350 Main Street, and Thelma Ann went to a girls' boarding school in Salt Lake City. The truth is she would have been smart even if she had gone to the Marsac grade school in Park City.

When she overheard me boasting about being a 12-pound baby born at home, Thelma Ann really humiliated me. She stepped forward and declared that the only way a baby that big could be born was with a Caesarean operation.

I asked what Caesarean meant, and she said it was some sort of operation named after Julius Caesar, the first person to be born that way. I thought that was great! Julius Caesar was some sort of old-time Roman who liked to sword fight and things like that. Hell, I couldn't go wrong with that. New bragging rights! I was in debt to Thelma Ann.

It was only a short time until my life came unraveled. It seemed my friends had questioned their parents and the majority opinion was that the only way a 12-pound baby could have been born would have been in a hospital. It's not fun having five or six good friends calling you a liar.

The author's mother, Maud Smith Kimball.
Photo courtesy of the Kimball Archive.

When I questioned my mother, she chuckled and then laughed with each animated gesture as she told me about my birth.

It seems that every normal child who was delivered at home by Doctor Harold I. Goodwin was a 12-pounder. Few homes in that day had bathroom scales. When asked for a weight, Doc Goodwin would go through a routine of placing the newborn in the palm of his hand and, with a studious look upon his face, would proclaim: "This child is a 12-pounder!" It did not vary. Every child that Doctor Goodwin delivered outside the hospital weighed 12 pounds.

This was the first time that I can remember questioning my mother's judgment. For me there was no humor in her story.

Many years later, while home on leave from the Navy, I had the honor of being Thelma Ann's date to her graduation dance at St. Mary of the Wasatch Academy. It was a fun night. She still liked correcting me when I didn't know what I was talking about – such as the time I claimed the singer on the radio was Ella Fitzgerald when it was Sarah Vaughan. I can close my eyes and still hear her laughing.

Big brothers were funny. Sometimes they were the greatest people in the world, helping you with homework or letting you tag along with them when fishing on the creek below town or going to the movies on Friday night. Of course, when we got to the movies, we would separate and I would find my friends to sit with.

Friday night at the movies was kids' night. They would have a cliffhanger serial, usually followed by a short film such as one by the Three Stooges, then a cartoon and a good cowboy movie.

Oh how I loved the serials. "The Phantom," "Gene Autry," "Captain America" and "The Scarlet Rider" were all great in my mind. When I got home I would have to tell Mom everything about the movie, not leaving out any details. On Saturday my friends and I would reenact the movie or serial in play.

Friday night was the only night during the school year that I could count on being able to go out. However, there were a few special events that happened on weeknights that I got to go to.

Once there was a minstrel show at the War Memorial Building (now Park City Live) that would never happen today. All the actors were white but had black greasepaint covering their faces

The three Kimball boys on the front porch of the family home at 655 Woodside Avenue. The author is the baby, with Paul behind him and Gib on the right. *Photo courtesy of the Kimball Archive.*

and wore loud checkered jackets and baggy pants. They told jokes and sang and danced to the banjo.

I think it was in conjunction with a war-bond rally, and the actors were probably Utahns. Instead of being on stage, they were seated in the balcony, which had tier seating, while the audience sat in folding chairs on the gym floor and looked up at them.

War-bond rallies were often held at the War Memorial Building. Usually they would show color movies of the war. Once, I remember, an armored car and a tank were parked in front of the building and we got to climb all over them.

If there were a lot of things going on in the Park, the old American Theatre, 356 Main Street, would be opened for special events. I remember one event when they erected a boxing ring on stage. Then they recruited as many boys of a similar weight as the ring could hold, or until they ran out of boxing gloves. When the bell sounded, everyone started punching. When a kid was knocked down, he was escorted from the ring, until only one kid remained standing. He was proclaimed the champion.

I don't remember being in the ring. I don't think it was because I was a coward, but rather because I really didn't know what they were doing until the punches started to fly. I think it was luck on my part for being dumb.

One of my memories of the American Theatre was watching my buddy Raymond Beckstead on stage. The performer – I wish I could remember his name – was great. He threw knives that came so close to hitting his girl assistant that the audience screamed, and he used a whip better than Lash LaRue of movie fame, putting out cigarettes that dangled from her lips.

He then balanced a ladder on his chin and called for a volunteer from the audience. Raymond got the honor. The performer looked Ray over and said, "You're too heavy. Take off your shoes."

If anything, Raymond was lighter than my 65 pounds.

"You're still too heavy. Take off your coat."

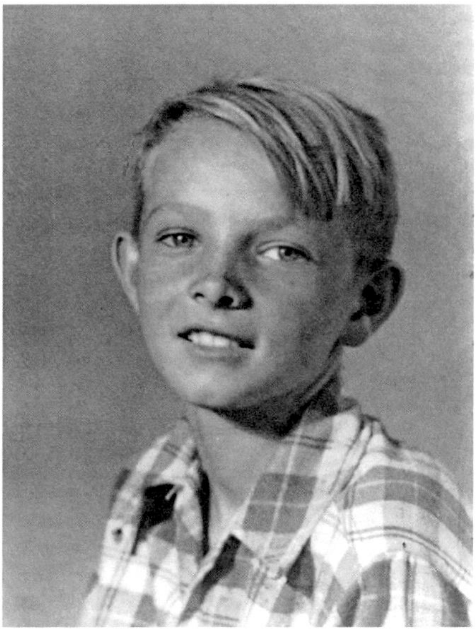

The author as he looked in the seventh grade.

By the time he was done, Raymond had only his pants left. Then the performer balanced Raymond on top of an eight-foot ladder balanced on his chin. I am still impressed.

Raymond was one of my best friends, although it seemed we spent a great deal of time arguing. It did not matter what subject came up or what I told him, he wouldn't believe it. His response was always, "Prove it!"

Ray was a year or so behind me in school. One frigid Friday night we were on our way to the movies and I was telling him about a great book my teacher was reading to her class.

The practice at the Marsac School, it seemed to me, was for the teachers to read a chapter or so of some novel each morning. Usually the books they chose were pulp juvenile novels. This novel (I have forgotten its title) was about a boy and his dog that stowed away on a ship bound for an Arctic expedition. When the weather turned cold, they had to leave their hiding place in a lifeboat in search of a warmer place to hide. Somehow, during their move, the dog happened to lick the railing and got his tongue stuck to it.

Raymond challenged me to prove such an outlandish thing could happen. The idea of getting a tongue stuck on anything Ray would not accept.

Our argument started at the bottom of Main Street and continued up to the Central Drug Store at 411 Main Street. He kept telling me to prove it, and I kept telling him that, if he could find

Raymond Beckstead as a high school sophomore. *Photo courtesy of Park City High School 1952 yearbook.*

a dog, I'd do my best to get it to lick some frozen metal.

That wouldn't do for him; he challenged me to lick a light post or something metal. I wouldn't do it. I told him I believed the book. And besides, if it didn't work, he'd win the argument.

Finally, Raymond said he would prove me wrong. Whereupon he stuck his tongue on the metal pole that supported the drug-store sign.

I won the argument. Raymond ripped a chunk of skin off his tongue and bled like a stuck pig. He was mad as hell at me for letting him do it. No matter what I said or how sorry I was, it was my fault. He was so mad that he went home without seeing the movie. And it was at least a week before he would speak to me.

As I said earlier, big brothers are strange. At times they are the neatest people around, helping you do homework or showing you the proper way to color with crayons, and sometimes they let you tag along. But at other times they can be awful tricky.

Once, when my brother Gibby had to tend me – he called it babysitting – he told me that I would light up like a light bulb if I put my thumb in a socket. I climbed up on the kitchen table, unscrewed the ceiling light and followed his advice. God! I don't know if I lit up or not, but I did see colors, and I gained a healthy respect for electricity.

At one time I used to love Wheaties, "Breakfast of Champions," until Gibby looked at a bowl of Wheaties I was eating, pointed to an odd-shaped flake and said, "Look, you've got a grasshopper leg floating in there!" I haven't eaten Wheaties again to this day because of that.

Then there's the time he shot me – or for a while I thought he did. Again he was supposed to be watching me while I played in the backyard with friends. He had a 12-gauge shotgun that had been modified to the point that it was illegal. It had a sawed-off barrel and a stock that had been replaced with a homemade pistol grip.

Gibby had removed the pellets and wadding from a shell and loaded the gun. Hanging out of the upstairs window, he called for me to come closer. When I was about 15 feet away, he pulled out the shotgun, aimed at me and said, "You're dead!"

BOOM!

A flash of fire came roaring towards me, followed by a lot of smoke. I thought I'd been shot and fell backward, but wondered why it didn't hurt. I was afraid to move for fear I would start hurting.

When my hearing returned, all I could hear was Gibby laughing. Pretty soon my playmates started laughing and demanding to be shot too. But just like big brothers everywhere, once you start having fun with them, they quit playing.

One time I pooled my cash with Raymond and we purchased a 15-cent kite from Oblad's 5 & 10-cent store at 436 Main Street. We did a great job of assembling it and took it down on the railroad tracks where there were no trees or telephone poles or wires to interfere with it. Unfortunately, there was not enough wind either. Try as we might, we couldn't get the damn thing off the ground.

About then Gibby and his pal Hal Himes came along. They were on their way to do a little shooting on Masonic Mountain (now better known as the Aerie and covered in houses). Each of them had a .22 rifle in hand, and Gibby was all smiles. He told us that if we wanted to get the kite off the ground we should come with them; the wind was always strong on top of the mountain. We jumped at the offer and, sure enough, within a few minutes the kite was soaring 60 feet in the sky.

Gibby suggested it would be great fun and would sharpen our skills as shooters if we were to use the kite as a target.

It was a great suggestion. I had only once fired a gun, when Dad took me with him to the old rifle range in Deer Valley, and I doubt if Raymond had ever fired one.

No sooner had we approved his plan than Gibby and Hal let loose with a torrent of fire. Within a minute, what was left of our beautiful orange kite had come crashing to earth. I was on the verge of tears when Gibby handed me his rifle and I got a chance to shoot at the skeleton of the kite. Raymond and I each took a half-dozen shots, and we were happy as sin.

To help in the war effort, nearly everyone in town had a Victory Garden. The mining company loaned property just east of the Spiro Tunnel to anyone in the city who wanted to plant a garden but didn't have property of their own to use.

In the latter part of summer, many of us kids would raid these gardens. It was a grand sport. Children who refused to eat fresh fruit and vegetables at home would devour their ill-gotten gains with glee. Parents would have been in a state of shock if they could have witnessed their children's furious appetites.

One good thing that the war did was to help change Park City's curfew law. Before then they blew the City Hall whistle at 9 p.m. and children under 12 had to be home. Then, during the war, the federal government imposed Daylight Saving Time on the nation. But in summer it was still daylight at 9 p.m. and many parents complained, so the City Council changed the curfew to 10 p.m. and left it that way even when the nation went back to standard time.

During the summer break from school, one of my oldest friends, Jimmy Jennings, would come to town. Jimmy spent most of the war years at the Japanese internment camp at Topaz, Utah. His father, who had experience as a Civilian Conservation Corps (CCC) administrator, was assigned to Topaz. Jimmy and his sister Freddie (Winifred) went to school with the interned Japanese children.

I thought Jimmy was brave to do this, but he just shrugged and said that many of them were good friends and were teaching him how to speak Japanese. He could already count to ten in Japanese and taught me: "Ichi, ni, san, shi, go, roku, shichi, hachi, kyuu, juu."

I was real proud of myself, but afraid to show off too much. I didn't want anyone thinking I was Japanese and sending me to live in Keetley (the site of a self-imposed Japanese relocation camp in Wasatch County) during the war.

One time, when Jimmy came to town, Mom wouldn't let me go outside to play. A week or so earlier, while exploring the city's trash dump, I had followed my companions through a smoldering ash pile. They got through OK, but for some reason I didn't. I guess they stirred up the ashes and the ashes relit, or my pant leg "floated" on top of the ashes as my leg sank in. Anyway, I got a serious burn on my right calf.

I was really afraid of what my parents would do if they discovered I had been at the trash pile, so I said nothing to anyone about it. For several days I limped around the house until Mom demanded I take off my shoes and stockings so she could inspect my feet.

I almost got away with it. She found nothing wrong with my feet, but she watched as I put on my stockings and saw me wince in pain when I pulled the right one up. She discovered the cluster of huge blisters that encircled my leg nearly to the knee. It triggered her into action. We didn't have a phone, so she sent my brother Paul to the neighbors to have them phone the doctor.

Doctors back in those days actually made house calls. It was only a short wait until Dr. Goodwin was at the door. He lanced all the blisters, covered the whole burn with some sort of ointment, and wrapped my leg. He gave me a good lecture about the dangers of playing around the "city dump."

Every point he made, my mother reinforced with, "You better be listening to him!" or, "Do you hear what he saying?" or, "If I ever hear you've been even near that dump, you'll never leave this house again!" But I was delighted that she wasn't as mad as I thought she'd be.

Anyway, Mom wouldn't let me out of the house until my burn was completely healed. So when Jimmy came to visit, I had to stay in, but she let us play "upstairs."

The upstairs room was Dad's trophy room, where he kept his collection of guns, knives, swords, gas masks and helmets. Most of this stuff was from WWI. Most he acquired when he operated the Kimball Service Station. During the Depression, many customers would give Dad such items to hold until they had cash to pay him for the tank of gas, but some never returned to redeem their trophies.

Jimmy Jennings as a high school freshman. *Photo courtesy of Park City High School 1952 yearbook.*

The upstairs was a great place to play. It had always been off limits to me. It also served as my brother Gibby's bedroom, but that week he was off to Orem, Utah, where he had a job picking cherries. That afternoon was almost worth the burn.

Jimmy was fun to play with. We all but won the war with our great inventions. One was a pill that, when you took it, turned into a full-fledged meal: a turkey dinner with all the trimmings, a T-bone steak with baked potatoes, or anything else you could imagine. We also invented a bomb that could destroy a city and really got mad a year or so later when the government stole our idea.

With the end of the war, Jimmy moved back to Park City, went through both Marsac Elementary School and Park City High School, then did a stint in the Navy. Somewhere along the way Jimmy became Jim and then James. He went on to earn a law degree. In 1983 he was appointed a judge to the Santa Maria Superior Court in California. Judge James Jennings had a long, distinguished career before he retired to Idaho.

Oscar, 'Government Trapper'

(Oscar Clegg, November 11, 1895 – April 6, 1950)

Oscar Clegg's son, Bobby, as a high school junior.
Photo courtesy of Park City High School 1955 yearbook.

This is the first time I have written anything about any of my friends' parents. For most of the period covered by this sketch I was nine to eleven years of age. I thought most of my friends' parents were OK, but I learned early on that parents were to be avoided. Most were like my parents. They always wanted to know where you were going, what you were going to do, and had a lot of other dumb questions I didn't have answers for.

It seemed all my friends would brag about their dads. They were the strongest, the toughest, and smarter than anyone else's dad.

Of course, they didn't know what they were talking about, 'cause my dad was the best and bravest.

And then there was the challenge: "When my dad gets home from work, I'm going to have him beat up on your dad!"

When challenged like that, I would have to accept, but then I would worry that some angry father might really come knocking at our door. It wasn't that I was worried that my dad would lose, but I'm sure he would have been mad at me for spoiling his evening.

He had what I think is called a routine. He didn't call it that, but I know that after supper he would settle down in his easy chair with his newspaper. He hated being disturbed, and usually after a short time would fall asleep.

I don't remember anyone calling his father "father." Usually, the term used when addressing him was "dad." When we got older, most of us used the third-person term "the old man" – when he wasn't around, that is.

I had one friend whose father I held in high esteem, and that was Bobby Clegg. He actually called his dad "Pa," and right to his face.

Bobby's dad, Oscar, was one of a kind. He was as big as the professional wrestler Man Mountain Dean. A salt-and-pepper two-day growth of beard seemed perpetual. His usual attire was bib overalls and a long-sleeve western-cut shirt. He billed himself as a "government trapper."

In looking back, I have no idea where this self-proclaimed title came from or exactly what it meant. My best guess is that it was because he collected bounties on animals the government considered a threat to man or livestock. Most of the time he wasn't around. He was in the mountains, or out in the Uinta Basin, hunting, trapping or prospecting.

When Oscar returned home, he'd be driving a Model T Ford, but not always the same one. Sometimes it was a Model T pickup truck, other times a sedan, once a coupe that had a rumble seat. Once, Bobby and I got to ride in that seat down the "old back road" (the extension of Norfolk Avenue that was platted but never constructed due to avalanche danger) and up Main Street to the Post Office. Another time we got to ride in the back of the pickup truck and almost got bounced out on the old back road.

I don't know where Oscar found these cars; each seemed older and more beat-up than its predecessor. When his car was broken down, he would always find a ride out to the Uinta Basin using one story or another.

Once, when my dad showed an interest in the capstones that Oscar had placed on his stone wall facing Woodside Avenue, Oscar told him he'd show him where he could find more of the same rocks, and he could scout some good deer-hunting country at the same time.

The so-called rocks were petrified wood! Most were huge, weighing close to two hundred pounds each. Neither Bobby nor I could budge them, even when we worked together. Anyway, Dad drove Oscar and my brother Gibby out to the Uinta Basin the following weekend. On the way out, Oscar would find one reason or another to check some side canyon. It finally dawned on Dad that they were checking Oscar's traps. He trapped most anything that paid a bounty: bear, wolf, coyote, and a whole host of other varmints.

Dad did bring home a couple of pieces of petrified wood, but they weren't much to look at. I think he was disgusted by the whole trip. Bobby later told me that his pa knew where there was a whole forest of nothing but petrified stuff – not just trees, but animals too, like a squirrel that got petrified while climbing up a tree.

Oscar really could tell a good tale, and if you were lucky enough to be there when he was talking, it was fun just to be quiet and listen. The only person who didn't seem impressed was Della,

Bobby's mom. She would listen for a little while, then roll her eyes a certain way and walk off.

Bobby paid no mind; he'd listen intently and try to copy his pa's pattern of speech, and his mannerisms.

When Oscar had a runny or stuffed-up nose, he didn't use a handkerchief. Instead, he'd place his thumb over one nostril and then blow with all his might. With a mighty snorting sound a snot missile would sail forth 10 feet or more into the yard.

It was a feat we all tried to copy, but most of us would give up after a few attempts. Not Bobby. He kept at it for months. In fact, I bet to this day, when no one is around, he is still trying to get it right. I think from that time on, a runny nose was part of Bobby's makeup.

When it came to bears, Bobby became our expert. He would say with authority, "There are polar bears, brown bears, cinnamon bears, black bears, grizzly bears, but the biggest, meanest, and a real man-eater is the BEAAR!" He exaggerated the pronunciation just as his pa did.

We'd tell him that there ain't no such thing as a Beaar. But Bobby wouldn't hear of any such thing. His pa said it, so it was true! Bobby would then go into great detail about how his father caught one in a trap, emptied his gun on it, and then had to use an ax to finish the job.

As the years passed, I heard several versions of the story. The most popular one was that, believing he would find the trap empty, Oscar had left his rifle in the truck, but carried the ax to help reset the trap if it had sprung. Not wanting to walk a half-mile back to the truck, he decided he could kill the bear with the ax and discovered he was in for a fight. Under those circumstances, I can see how a black bear might become a giant BEAAR.

The Cleggs' house at 615 Woodside Avenue was once a boardinghouse that had been converted into three apartments. However, most of the time Oscar had no renters. With World War II ending,

Park City's mining boom had slackened to a much slower pace. The lack of renters put the Clegg family in a financial bind. Times were tough for many Park City families.

In Oscar's backyard were several buildings. There was a long, low-lying building that housed three or four coalhouses/storages sheds. Just north of the sheds was a larger wood structure that Oscar used to store his gear. It was locked most of the time. It held a variety of steel-claw traps ranging from the huge three-foot-long bear traps, that took both Bobby and me to lift, to the small eight-inch traps used on rabbits and other small varmints. There was a block-and-pulley suspended from the rafters for hanging fresh kills.

Other than a whole lot of empty boxes, there wasn't much to look at or play with in there. Besides, the place stunk of old hides, mostly deer hides that he had bought from local hunters who were lucky enough to bag deer.

One year Dad got lucky on the elk hunt and bagged a big buck. He gave me the hide that had been cut into three equal sections. I sold them to Oscar for three dollars each. It was the most money I ever had to spend on Christmas presents. I really thought I was rich.

Once, when Oscar left the door unlocked, Bobby found what he was looking for. After a moment in the building, he stepped into the sunlight holding a quart jar that was three-quarters full and said, "I found it! This is Pa's coyote scent!"

"What's coyote scent?" I asked.

"It's the stuff you pour on the trap – so coyotes won't smell you."

I sniffed myself. "I don't stink. Why would a coyote think I smell?"

Bobby look disgusted. "They won't go near any trap that smells like a human."

I asked, "What's it smell like?"

"I don't know," he said. "Pa said to keep my hands off it or there would be hell to pay."

Well, I gave him one of those "I dare you" looks and he couldn't resist. He got a good grip on the bottle with his left hand and, with his right hand, twisted the lid with all his might.

Bobby was pretty strong and the lid came off easily. He took a sniff. The next thing I knew, with his eyes shut, holding the jar up as high as he could reach, he started coughing ... and dropped the jar.

I knew, even before the jar splintered into a hundred pieces, what was in it. It was SKUNK!

Now I knew what skunk smelled like, but I never knew it could be this bad. Some of it splashed on Bobby when the jar broke. His eyes were all red and he was beginning to cry.

"We got to cover the stink before Pa gets home!"

I began to cough and my eyes were running. "I don't think you can," I said. I emphasized the "*you*" so he'd know that I didn't have anything to do with *his* accident.

He asked, "Do you think Pa will smell it?"

"Maybe not," I lied.

Bobby was sobbing aloud as he turned and walked slowly toward his mother who had caught a whiff of the offensive odor and was staring at us from the back porch. I didn't realize I had been running until a few minutes later when I was safe in my room.

A short while later I learned the truth about the so-called coyote scent. It really was skunk musk, and it was used on traps, not only to cover human scent but also hopefully to prevent the coyote from stealing the game caught in the trap.

I'm not sure what kind of punishment Bobby got. It was quite a while before I ventured into his neighborhood. Eventually he and I started playing together again. But I do know for a fact that that particular piece of land stunk for years, and I mean years.

Fifteen or 20 years later you could still pick up the odor if you sniffed hard enough!

Bobby's mother, Della, didn't like him going to the Friday night movie. She didn't like him on Main Street at night. I could go if I was with one of my brothers, but that was no fun.

They'd have the same movie on Saturday afternoon, so often I'd go with Bobby. We loved going to the Egyptian Theatre. They always played a serial – usually a western like "The Scarlet Rider" – as well as a cartoon, a preview of coming movies, and then the main movie.

The main movie usually was a cowboy film; sometimes it would star Gene Autry, who would sing. I guess that was for the girls who went to the movies. Most of us thought girls should not be allowed to see cowboy movies. Then maybe they would do away with such nonsense as singing.

Afterwards we would reenact what we had seen, with each boy "dubbing" the actor he wanted to be. Bobby was fast at this. "I dubs to be the Scarlet Rider," he would shout as we exited the movie house. Sometimes we argued over this.

"The Scarlet Rider" was a good serial, and everyone wanted to be the star. It would last 12 episodes, which gave us many adventures. Somewhere Bobby found an old sheet so we could fix up a costume to look something like The Scarlet Rider.

By this time my big brother Gib had told me that scarlet was nothing but another name for the color red, and that in reality they were trying to steal the name from "The Red Rider." You couldn't really tell what color was what from watching a black-and-white movie, and I didn't want to believe my brother. I didn't know much about using a dictionary so I spent a whole evening trying to disprove him. Damn it, he was right again.

It didn't matter, because by the time we put on our costumes it was dark, and no one would know what color they were. We were going to put the fear of the Scarlet Rider into them, no matter what!

Where the Crescent Tramway meets Park Avenue, we put on our costumes with nervous anticipation, picturing the people we would scare. We ran down Park Avenue, howling like wolves to get people's attention.

Running as fast as I could, I ran into a wire gate left open at Don Peterson's house.

WHAM!

It's funny how you can see colors in the dark! It knocked me off my feet and cut my lip. Before I could get back on the Tramway, the face part of my costume had turned scarlet!

One time, after the matinee, we stopped at the Central Drug Store. It was the only place in town that sold comic books, and Doc Gordon had a good soda fountain. There was nothing in the world better that a 10-cent comic book and a five-cent fountain drink to keep a person happy. I don't remember how we came into this surplus capital, but we spent it wisely.

While trying to decide which fountain drink to order, Doc Gordon, in a friendlier tone than usual, said, "Have you boys ever tried a 'Wild Injun' soda?"

"No," we answered in unison.

"Why, I'll fix one now, and it will be on the house."

You can't go wrong with a deal like that. I was not sure what he put in it, but I know he added a squirt of this, and a squirt or that, then a double squirt of what I'm quite sure was lemon extract, then filled the rest up with fountain water.

Wow! It was sour! Oh how we loved it!

"Yap, a 'Wild Injun,' a drink only served in the Central Drug Store in Park City, but you have to be tough to drink it!" Doc Gordon proclaimed.

Well, I guess we bragged about that drink a little too much around Oscar. One afternoon, Bobby asked his pa if he could have a nickel so he could go uptown with me and have a Wild Injun. Oscar didn't get upset or anything. He just said he could make a sourer, fizzier drink at home, and it wouldn't cost us a thing.

I knew that was impossible, and even Bobby looked at his father with questioning eyes. Oscar, without saying a word, walked into the kitchen, put about a half teaspoon of baking soda into a glass, filled it up about halfway with water, gave it a little stir with a spoon and added a lid full of vinegar. Presto! You actually could hear the fizzing glass from six feet away. Oscar gave us a "see, I told you so" look as he drank his "Vinegar Fizz" down.

Now Bobby was clamoring for his pa to make him one. I watched, but didn't say a word. Secretly I was hoping I'd get one too.

We must have had at least three apiece before Della broke up our party.

It was beginning to get dark when I got ready to go home. As I was leaving, Oscar said, "Pay no attention if you hear what sounds like a baby cryin' up on the mountain."

I guess I had a puzzled look on my face because he added, "There's a bobcat up there and he sounds just like a baby cryin'. It's his way of trickin' people, especially boys and girls, to go lookin' for that cryin' child. And they say the smart ones can throw their cries so you don't know where the sound is comin' from, and it could be right behind you."

As Oscar told me this he stared at Treasure Mountain, then quickly glanced over his shoulder, then back at me.

It seemed that every time I left the Cleggs' house after that, I would get home faster than the time before. I think I had it down to less than 90 seconds. For a while, whenever it was dark, I could hear a baby crying and the sound, though distant, seemed to be coming from everywhere.

Now I have seen bobcat tracks, and know people who've said they had seen one in the wild, but I'm not one of them. The only person I know who supposedly shot one was Park City Marshal Frank Marcellin. And it turned out not to be a bobcat at all, just an extremely large tomcat with its tail cut off. But still, when it's dark and I hear a baby crying, I usually head for home.

Oscar was one of a kind – a throwback to the 19th century – and he really enjoyed playing this type of joke on the kids in the neighborhood. It was seldom anyone could get the best of him.

However, I remember once when someone did. Back in the 1940s there was an AM radio station that broadcast from "the Republic of Mexico." Its call letters were XELO. It probably had the strongest signal in the Western Hemisphere. At night it was easy to find on the dial. A business in the small border town of Clint, Texas, was a large advertiser on the station.

One ad caught Oscar's attention. It proclaimed that its "Insect Eliminator ... is guaranteed to kill all insects or double your money back. Only two dollars."

Well, Oscar could not resist this offer and sent off a money order to Clint, Texas. A week or so later an impatient Oscar received his Eliminator, and it worked as the directions said it would.

It consisted of two pieces of wood. One had a large X printed in the center; the other piece was shaped like a paddle. Written on it were these words: "Place insect on X and hit with paddle."

Oscar cussed a long, cruel oath and told his wife not to talk about this to anyone. But Della, who seldom found humor in anything, took delight in warning everyone she knew about the scam being operated out of Clint, Texas.

"Don't tell anybody," she said. "It got Oscar."

Bobby had two brothers who were much older than he was. I think the oldest was Hap; he served in the Coast Guard in World War II. After the war he married a girl from Kamas, Utah, and moved there. He got a job in the mines and commuted back and forth. I never really got to know him.

Sometime in the mid-1940s, Bobby's other brother, Ray, his wife Edith and their son Jimmy moved into one of the upstairs apartments.

Jimmy was about five years of age, maybe six, about two years younger than us, but a lot of fun to play with. When we were reenacting a Red Rider movie, no one ever wanted to play the part of Beaver, the little Indian kid. But Jimmy didn't mind at all. In fact, he thought it was great, and I have to admit he was good. His homemade bow and arrow even worked better than our cap pistols.

Jimmy's mother, Edith, was the adopted daughter of Epsy George, who lived next door to the north of my home. Edith also was related to the Hall family that lived up on Park Avenue. The Halls had a son, Kim, who was Jimmy's age. It was fun having younger kids around that kinda thought you knew what you were doing.

Ray was a good Mormon. In fact, almost all the Cleggs were religious, although I'm not really sure about Oscar. Anyway, Ray and family hadn't been living there long when he got a "call" to serve as the bishop to the Mormon First Ward (congregation).

The family was thrilled; Della was beside herself with pride. I guess it's only natural that Bobby and Jimmy wanted to get in on it. Bobby got the idea that we should write his brother a letter congratulating him.

Well, we kind of forgot what the letter was for. Besides, scary letters are more fun and use words that are easier to spell. I can't remember exactly what we wrote, but we called him "Bishop" and told him "to prepare to die at 13 o'clock" on the day he was taking the position. We thought "13 o'clock" was really funny.

Saturday night we slipped the letter under the apartment door and waited. Nothing happened. I thought the next day we would hear something, but we didn't. So I forgot all about it.

But Ray didn't think it was funny. I guess it scared the hell out of him! He called the police, they called the FBI, and this triggered an investigation. I soon discovered they didn't know how to take a joke. They wanted to catch this anti-Mormon-commie-pinko in the worst way and use him to set an example.

Park City was never what you would call a Mormon town. In fact, it's still the gentile capital of Utah. I didn't know any of this back then.

I understand they brought in handwriting experts to profile someone who had the ability to write in the manner of a child, and to analyze the meaning of the note, if any.

It was Della who solved the case. She knew Bobby and, with one hard look, caused him to burst into tears. He, of course, blamed me for forcing him and Jimmy to go along.

All was forgiven and, to show I was no commie or whatever it was they hated, I started, for a time, going to church with Bobby.

Negro Hollow

Illustration of Jenks Nelson by Don Weller.

Much of this story I used as an introduction to "What's In Name?" – the third story in my book, "Life under China Bridge". That was a protest of the Treasure Mountains resort's decision to change the historic name "Negro Hollow" to "Treasure Hollow" back in 1963 to please the customer base when neither the customers nor the resort knew the facts. In essence, it's a long and perhaps boring argument that in all likelihood found a small audience. I decided to recycle that introduction in this book with the promise to the reader to withhold the use of footnotes.

My childhood memories of Negro Hollow are of a beautiful place, a spacious opening surrounded by quaking aspen, with a few pine trees scattered throughout. Higher on the mountainsides that surrounded the hollow were scrub-oak trees that would take on various shades of red during the autumn season. There were several springs that attracted numerous species of butterflies, others insects and birds.

The evidence of wildlife was always abundant. You could always find tracks of deer and large cats if you were diligent in your search. At times, a good imagination would come in handy.

A large redwood water tank, which stood about six or seven feet high and about ten feet in diameter, had been constructed to supply water to the Glenwood Cemetery. After the cemetery hooked up to the city's water system, the tank and its system were soon forgotten. But even after years of neglect, the tank ran full and icy water slopped over the top. On occasion we would try to swim in it, but the water was too cold, and none of us wanted to be caught without pants or shoes if "Jenks" Nelson showed up.

To avoid a confrontation with Jenks, who owned Negro Hollow, all of us kids and most everyone else would enter the hollow by following the roadbed of the abandoned Crescent Tramway. (The tramway was a narrow-gauge railroad that once ran from lower Main Street – about where Marriott's Summit Watch villas are located today – and traversed the mountains until it reached the Crescent Mine above Thaynes Canyon.) At the point where the tramway made a sharp turn to the west was a well-used trail that led down to the hollow. At one point it skirted an abandoned mine whose portal was still intact.

I can't remember how many times my friends and I explored this mine tunnel. Once, when my buddy Ray Beckstead and I entered it, we heard a rustling sound and thought for sure it was a mountain lion. We skedaddled home for flashlights and weapons. We returned with a small army of kids ranging in age from about 10 to 13 armed with two .22 rifles, three BB guns, one bow-and-arrow, several clubs, a couple of candles and three flashlights. Alas, we were too late. The beast had escaped. Perhaps it was waiting for us perched high in a tree, ready to spring.

On other occasions the mine was not so frightening. There were two short side tunnels, one on the left and another on the right, each about 10 feet long. The main tunnel ran straight back, almost due south, for about 150 feet or so, then opened into a large room. There was a shaft in the center and the tunnel continued on.

The shaft was deep; it took five seconds for a tossed-in rock to hit the bottom, and its opening took up most of the room. A narrow ledge about 10 inches wide ran around the right side and could be used to reach the ongoing tunnel. But no one had the courage to walk it, no matter how many double-dares they got.

From time to time, when one of us found a long plank, we would carry it to the mine and try to span the opening. I have no idea how much wood we dropped down that shaft before we gave up, but it was enough to have built a great clubhouse. We were convinced the tunnel – it was going in the right direction, after all – would lead directly to the abandoned Creole Mine. If so, we would have had the world's greatest hiding place.

Jenks (William H.) Nelson was the only member of his family still living. He had outlived his parents, two brothers and three sisters, and was one salty, tough, old eccentric. It was exciting to watch him ride his horse up Main Street, ramrod straight in the saddle; he looked grand dressed in his World War I khaki uniform. The light posts along Main Street served as his hitching posts, and God pity anyone who looked at his horse the wrong way.

We lived in fear that Jenks would catch us in the hollow. Older kids told tales of his shooting at them with a shotgun loaded with buckshot. Every time we heard a muffled explosion, we ran for our lives, convinced the next shot might find its mark.

During this era the mines were operating full time, and the hollow was just a mile or so from the Silver King Mine. Blasting sounds were common. But don't tell that to a twelve-year-old in full flight.

Now, if we had bothered to read *The Park Record* newspaper, we would have been aware that many groups used the hollow as a meeting place from time to time. Various fraternal organizations and church groups such as the Mormon Mutual Improvement Association and the Catholic Youth Organization, along with class reunions, the Boy Scouts and even the Ladies Athenaeum would take delight in outings there. Hell, even my own Scout troop had a cookout there several times each summer. In hindsight, I know our Scoutmaster, Ken Webb, would have never planned those trips if permission was not forthcoming. I guess forbidden fruit always tastes better, and it was fun to be scared.

I was the only one in my group of friends who had been in Jenks's house. My family and the Nelsons had been friends from the time Colonel John A. Nelson and family arrived in the Park in the 1870s. Jenks and his brother Johnny were pallbearers at my grandfather's funeral in 1934. My father had stored the last of the Kimball Brothers stagecoaches in Jenks's barn for years.

The reason for my visit to his ranch was that Laverne, a schoolteacher friend of my mother from California, wanted to see the stagecoach. After inspecting the coach, we were invited into Jenks's home. It was grand: a marble-topped dresser and tables, laced sheer curtains beneath heavy maroon-colored drapes, and many ornate framed photos lining the walls, well lit by crystal-shaded lights. In one room, a whole wall was nothing but shelves filled with leather-bound books.

Jenks brought out a well-worn photo album that my mother and Laverne studied with care. Then he handed Laverne an 18-inch black braided hairpiece.

"Oh, your mother's hair!" exclaimed Laverne.

The last of the Kimball Brothers stagecoaches as it looked in a Park City parade in 1916. The man on the left holding the reins is Robert Taylor Kimball, the author's grandfather. The stagecoach was stored for many years in the Nelson barn. Now restored, it is on display in the Park City Museum.

"Hell no! That's an Injun scalp my pa took off a dead Injun after a skirmish in Montana."

Well, Laverne let out a scream that kinda sounded like a war-whoop to my ears and tossed the scalp the length of the room. As Jenks retrieved his artifact, you could hear him muttering something about that being no way to treat the dead.

I thought I had some great bragging rights based on that visit. But my friends thought I should take them to the ranch to play on the stagecoach. Well, I was not comfortable with that idea. I doubted if Jenks would have tolerated it. I know my dad would not have approved. So I never mentioned it again.

One experience in the hollow sticks out in my mind. One afternoon in late autumn, Bobby Clegg and I went there to do some shooting. I had my brother's pump .22 rifle and Bobby had a single shot .22. Tippy, Bobby's dog, was with us.

In reality, Tippy was kind of a joint-ownership dog. He had more or less moved into our home. Bobby's father had recently passed away. In the grieving and turmoil that followed, Tippy was neglected. He didn't desert the Cleggs; for a while he split his time evenly, but gradually came to be our dog. He was a grand dog, a malamute mix that bayed at the moon and loved the cold.

Maybe Tippy had a little bird dog in him too, for on this particular day he was great. We scared up some grouse that took flight so fast they were just a blur. Some landed in a tree ahead of us. We couldn't see them and would have just passed by, but Tippy stood stubbornly at the base of the tree, looking up, and would not move. So we studied the tree until we spotted what had been so apparent to the dog.

We shot three sage hens. Ah, the pride. We didn't know what kind of birds they were, but we knew they were big enough to be some kind of game birds.

Instead of taking the trail back up to the Crescent Tramway, we cut straight down through Nelson's ranch to Park Avenue and marched up the street in what some might have called a dance, carrying the birds high so that anyone else on the street would be sure to see them.

On reaching home, Bobby decided he didn't want his share of the birds. I didn't mind. The more for my family, I thought. It hadn't dawned on me that the old family edict now applied to me: "You shot it, you clean it, and you skin it!"

Well, I had cleaned a number of fish in my life, and one or two rabbits, and had seen deer skinned and cleaned. But Mom informed me you do not skin birds. You pluck their feathers by immersing the birds in hot water and then pulling out each feather. So I set up shop in the backyard on the platform where Mom hung her laundry.

Did I mention that it was late fall? As soon as the sun dipped behind Treasure Mountain, the temperature dropped. It was cold! The steam rolled off the tub of scalding water, mixing with the ungodly odor of wet feathers.

I pulled out feathers by the handful. They stuck to my hands, my clothing and even my hair. Suppressing shivers, I cursed Bobby, I cursed the dog, I cursed the hollow, and even my mother and the birds. Oh, did I curse birds, all birds!

My family seemed to enjoy the dinner my mother prepared. My dad was late getting home from work and did not see the evidence of my handiwork. His only remark was, "I hope they're in season."

As far as I was concerned, it was the end of an ugly episode – or so I thought until the next day, when I received a phone call. The caller identified himself as Judd Flinders, the game warden.

Flinders owned a farm down by Kimball Junction on the highway to Coalville and was engaged in a number of activities: farmer, restaurateur, operator of a children's commercial fishing pond, sod grower, real-estate developer, Mormon bishop and part-time game warden.

The caller explained that he had heard I had killed several grouse, which could result in the loss of the gun and a fine of $25 or so.

He went on with his lecture, but I missed most of what he said. A cold chill had settled over me. I felt a panicky urge to hide. I thought, Oh God, oh God, what will my parents do? What will I do?

Well, I did what I always did when a decision was needed. I did nothing.

My partner in crime, Bobby Clegg, got the same call. He panicked and told his mother all about our hunting trip. Bobby's mother, a recent widow with few resources, telephoned Warden Flinders to plead for her son.

I don't know what Flinders thought or what he said. I suspect he was puzzled by the phone call. I'm thankful he never took any action – or at least none we ever heard of.

Several days later I discovered what had really happened. Ray Sanchez, a kid a year older than me who possessed a devious sense of humor, had seen us marching past his house carrying our trophies. Ray had an awful deep voice for a 14-year-old. Oh, the delight he took in retelling the story about phoning us. It grew with each retelling. First, he said, he heard sniffles; in time, they became outright bawling. And he was sure that through the phone lines he could see the tears in our eyes.

In truth, I came away with a distaste for birds. Since then I have never eaten any game birds, I don't care much for chicken, and I only tolerate turkey on holidays.

Bobby remained a good friend, but I believe that was the last time we visited the hollow together. After I graduated from high school, we went separate ways. I went to college in Salt Lake for a year and then joined the Navy. Bobby married, divorced, then joined the Marines, but was soon discharged due to bad knees from old football injuries.

Eventually I started calling Bobby "Bob." He married Connie Winn, a native of Park City and a good friend, and they moved to Salt Lake. Occasionally we meet and exchange stories about the good old days.

My First Pets

The author with his pet lamb that he named, of course, Mary. *Photo courtesy of the Kimball Archive.*

One thing pet owners have in common is that they all believe their pets are the brightest and best that ever lived. In that respect I'm not much different from these other ill-informed people.

My dealings with pets date back to the mid-1940s starting with animals that usually aren't classified as pets. Some were flops. My very first pet I brought home to raise, love and train was a frog that I caught in Frog Valley.

Back then this valley was quite different from what it is today. It was a vast swampy field just below where the Deer Valley Snow

Park ski lodge now stands on the lower part of the resort. At one time there was also a straight track for racing horses, and on the far north side was a rifle range.

The section that attracted kids was on the northwestern edge of the valley. There were several ponds of waist-deep water and the foundation of an old zinc mill.

Way over on the far eastern side were the remains of a concrete bunker where the Welch, Driscoll & Buck department store had a powder house to keep dynamite. The last time I looked, I could not find any trace of it. I suppose the present condominium management company doesn't know about the secret treasure that is supposed to be buried somewhere on the hill behind the powder house. If you don't believe me, read George A. Thompson's book, "Some Dreams Die."

Back in those days, most of us called this small valley Smith Field. Smith, I understand, owned a butcher shop on Main Street back in earlier times and had his slaughterhouse here. To us, Deer Valley was the neighborhood that straddled Heber Avenue from the bottom of Main Street and terminated where it opened into Smith Field.

The very first time I visited Deer Valley on my own, I rode my tricycle there. I guess I was around five years old. As I think back on that trip, it was some sort of a feat for someone so young. The road was gravel with potholes galore. No sooner had I got there than it started to rain, and it turned into a heavy downpour. The ride home was mired with mishaps. The potholes now were miniature lakes that I kept getting stuck in. I have never been so wet and cold.

To top it off, the barking dogs in the Deer Valley neighborhood scared the hell out of me. As soon as I got out of the territory of one dog, another one would take its place. I guess a kid on a tricycle in a cloudburst for some reason doesn't agree with dogs.

By the time I got home, I was soaked to the bone. I got a good scolding from my mother for playing in the rain. She marched me into the bathroom and didn't stop scolding as she drew a hot bath. I didn't tell her where I had been, or what a great feat I had accomplished, not because I was modest, but because I had an aversion to spanking. So until now, other than a few close friends, you are the first to hear of this remarkable feat.

Well, I should get back to my frog. I really don't remember what took me to Deer Valley on that day, or much else about it, except that I brought home a frog in a tin can. Long story short, he didn't care much for me. It seemed every time I picked him up, he peed on me! I don't think there are many five- or six-year-old kids who would care for that.

All my friends were either jealous or bored, or something. Anyway, they didn't show much interest in my frog and all had better things to do.

I made a pet box from a wooden Hercules powder box. I tacked a screen over the top and left a corner loose that I could fasten tight with a hook for easy access. I kept it for several years, until it finally fell apart.

The Hercules boxes were originally used to ship dynamite to the mines. Each box had a picture of Hercules with a skin robe slung over one shoulder and a big club over the other shoulder. After they were empty, miners and other mine employees brought them home, where they served a variety of uses.

I've seen them used as shelves and nightstands. One creative use was to store food during the winter months at boardinghouses. They would be anchored outside next to a window, usually on the second floor. Most often, though, they were used for kindling wood to start the morning's fire.

Anyway, someone left the screen open at the home I had fixed for my frog, hoping he would escape. I now think it was my father,

Wooden Hercules powder (dynamite) boxes from the mines were repurposed in many ways. The author used one as a home for a variety of pets. Here, some neighborhood children are playing around one that has been converted into a wheelbarrow.

but I wouldn't put it past one of my brothers borrowing him for some weird reason. My frog disappeared in less than a week.

Not long after that, I got a toad as a pet. For the life of me I can't remember who gave him to me. I still had the box and all, exactly as the frog had left it. There was not much for me to do but enjoy my new companion.

I don't think I'd had him for an hour when my older brother Gibby came by and looked at him. He told me how lucky I was because toads made great pets. That is, if you don't mind getting warts all over your body. And I should be extra careful not to touch my nose because that's where toad warts really like to grow.

Well, I didn't want to get warts, especially on the nose. I already had two on the back of my right hand and, no matter how hard I tried, I couldn't get rid of them. First I tried a remedy that

I had heard somewhere: I painted them with red nail polish. That didn't work. My brother Paul told all my friends that I had spilled the nail polish on my hand while I was painting my toenails. It's really embarrassing having to take off your shoes and stockings during recess at school to prove you didn't paint your toenails.

Arvil Price, a classmate who lived on Daly Avenue up in Empire Canyon, told me he got rid of his warts by following the advice of an old witch who lived in my neighborhood. He couldn't remember her name or exactly where she lived, but said I'd know she was a witch when I met her. He said you had to take a clean handkerchief and do some stuff with it – he couldn't remember exactly what – and then bury it at midnight under a full moon.

This was scary stuff he was telling me: a witch in my neighborhood that no one seemed to know about, and staying up until midnight when there's a full moon! My parents made sure I was in bed by nine o'clock on weekdays, and weekends were not much better.

I don't think I told anyone about my search for the witch. I knew my parents would not approve, and my brothers ... well, I just knew they would tease me about it.

A search for a gray-haired old woman should be easy enough. For a while I was sure it was Rhea Hurley. She lived in a big old house just three houses up the Crescent Tramway from our home. She had gray hair, and was old, and mean. She kinda looked like the witches in the story books, and she hated kids playing around her house.

On occasion, when I was by myself, Rhea would ask me all kinds of questions about the goings-on at my house. Things like if my parents ever fought, and what kinds of things they talked about. I guess I wasn't much help to her. I hardly heard anything my parents said about anything, and she didn't want to hear about our fighting over the last piece of pie.

Anyway, she still had her son Patrick living at home, and a pretty good shepherd dog named Laddy, although the dog did spend more time at the Cullens' house. I guess the food was better there and there were more kids to bark at.

I finally decided she wasn't the witch. I felt bad about that because she would have made a good one. I looked at every other gray-haired woman in the neighborhood. I soon became convinced that Arvil was telling me a fib, or that it was a "ghost witch" that only people like Arvil could see. Then I remembered an old lady we bumped into on the way home from school the year before.

It was just north of the old Jefferson School on the trail we used to get from Park Avenue to Woodside Avenue. It was a neat shortcut that few, if any, grownups used. There, standing in the pathway, was an old lady who really amazed and scared us with her crazy talk. Thinking back, she could have been a witch.

She said she was a doctor and, way back when, she had actually saved George Washington's eyesight, and maybe even his life. She said it happened when he got shot in the corner of the eye. She just plucked the eye out, took out the bullet, put the eye back in place and gave him a pirate-patch to wear 'til it healed. She kept gesturing with her hands – kind of showing us how she did it – while she talked. I was afraid she wanted to demonstrate the operation on one of us.

I'm not sure which one of us started to run first, but I know I was not the last to leave, and it took a while for the rest of the gang to catch up to me. The idea of some old lady taking my eye out to show my friends how she did it to George Washington terrified me. I knew she was awful old, but I didn't think she was that old. Anyway, that was the only time I saw her, and it was the last time I used that shortcut for a long, long time. But I became sure she was Arvil's witch.

I decided I had to get rid of my pet toad, but that was turning into a big problem. Most of my friends now knew of the danger of getting warts from toads. Every time I just about had one of them convinced that toads were great, fun pets, one of my brothers would show up and ask something like, "You got any new warts – besides the ones you've already got?" I knew I had to do something sneaky to get rid of him, yet in doing so find him a good home.

⚒ ⚒ ⚒

One hot summer evening, my friend Ray Beckstead and I were catching nightcrawler worms to sell for fishing and caught way more than we could sell. We were in Art Workman's backyard, the back door to the kitchen was open, and Art and his family were all in the front room. There was only the screen door between the worms and a good joke.

I know we shouldn't have done it, but most of the can of worms we dumped on his kitchen floor were actually caught in his garden, and if you didn't think about it too much, it seemed proper.

Anyway, Art and his family were awful nice people and I was sure they would give the toad a real nice home.

It took me three nights of waiting until I could deliver my gift toad. After that I played around the Workmans' yard for several days, hoping to find out how the toad was doing, but no one said a word about him, and it wasn't long before I found new things to do.

What I really wanted was a "real" pet such as a dog or a cat, but I knew my parents would not hear of such a thing because of my first experience with a cat.

I guess I was about five years old, and I really liked playing with my next-door neighbor, Peggy Bircumshaw. She lived with her parents in a house my dad built and rented out. It was a small two-bedroom cottage, painted white. Peggy was a little younger than me and thought I was nice. I guess she was my first girlfriend.

On the south side of our house lived "Old Man Peterson" – that's what we called Mr. Peterson. He owned a big white cat that liked to come around; she loved being petted and other stuff that cats like. Peggy wondered why you never see blue, green or red cats. I thought that was a good question and set about finding out how a cat would like a new color.

In my dad's workshop – an extension at the back of the house that we all called the "playhouse" – I found a half-used can of green paint and a couple of stiff paintbrushes. With a little work, I soon had the lid off the can.

All this time, Peggy was petting the cat. When she saw the paint can, her eyes grew big and she began to giggle, thinking about the fun we were going to have.

We both were dabbing our brushes into the paint when Bob Cullen showed up. Bob was two years older than me and lived just on the other side of Peggy's house. He was one of those take-charge-type older boys and knew immediately what we were up to. Saying, "You're doing it all wrong," he took the bucket and began to pour the paint onto the cat's now-arching back. In the blink of an eye, the once-white cat had vanished.

Well, we still had a fourth of a can of paint, and paintbrushes, and I guess both Bob and I wanted to impress Peggy. So we decided to paint her house. After all, it was kinda dull, just being a white house, and Peggy agreed it could use some color. We set to work on the southwest corner of the house and were really making progress when all hell broke loose.

There stood Old Man Peterson, with my mother. Peterson was shouting so loud that Peggy's mother came charging out of her house to see what was happening. Bob disappeared so fast that I'm not sure they knew he was there at all. Mrs. Bircumshaw, seeing Peggy – who was now crying and had almost as much paint on her as on her house – was really angry. They all focused their attention, or I should say anger, on me.

Mom kept saying, "Just wait until your father gets home!" I bet she said that a thousand times. She nearly pulled my arm off as she pointed me towards our back door and a bath. I got a spanking and was sent to bed.

Dad somehow made amends with Mr. Peterson. I'm not sure what became of his cat. She no longer came around our house. Mr. Peterson would shake his head every time he saw me. It seemed as though Peggy disappeared as well. I saw little of her after that. Then, for no reason at all, they moved away. It seemed like a long time before Bob Cullen would have anything to do with me.

After that, I knew it wouldn't do me any good to ask for a pet cat.

One day, while playing up near the second Creole Mine dump, Jim Jennings, Ray Beckstead and I stumbled upon a litter of baby cottontail rabbits. Each of us chased one down and we had pets that no one else in the neighborhood could boast of.

I'm not sure what became of Ray's bunny; I know it disappeared soon after capture. Anyway, he didn't talk about it.

Jim took his bunny to his grandfather's house. It was a neat house right next to the Silver King tramway. His grandfather, Doc Sheen, was the town's dentist. He was a fun yet wise man. He helped Jim fix a box house for his bunny and they placed it in their coal shed.

For the first couple of days, I worked hard feeding my bunny. Mom gave me a few carrots, but I had to find other things he liked to eat – such as dandelions and tall grass – and it was not very fun.

My brother Paul suggested I put my bunny on the lawn, with my upside-down pet box over him, so he could eat and mow the lawn at the same time. Well, it seemed like a good idea. Gathering dandelions and grass was getting a bit tiring, and Mom wouldn't part with any more carrots.

But even I could see a problem with his suggestion. Being under the box would put my baby bunny in the dark. I know I didn't like eating in the dark, so why would a bunny? Besides, it would mean taking the screen off the top of the box. It was hard enough putting it on; I was not about to take it off.

I came up with a better idea. I would tie a cord around one of the bunny's feet and tie the other end to a peg that I spiked into the ground. After watching him for a half-hour or so, I was convinced this was a great idea. I went to tell Jim about my great idea. Jim wanted to borrow some cord so he could do the same with his bunny.

Wouldn't you know it, when we got to my backyard, my bunny was gone! After I had turned my back on him, he had chewed through the cord. I should have known better. I knew rabbits made lousy pets, but the excitement of catching that bunny was fun, and I really thought we would be great friends. I really felt betrayed.

I should have mentioned that this wasn't my first experience with rabbits. My dad had a coop with a few chickens and several rabbits. One Easter Sunday, when I was about four years old, I jumped out of bed early expecting good things. What did I find? Nothing but a few colored hard-boiled eggs.

But my parents and brothers encouraged me to search the house to see what else I could find. Well, sure enough, in the bottom drawer of my chest-of-drawers was a very large, very white, pink-eyed rabbit.

I thought it was a stuffed toy. I grabbed it and gave it a big hug. The rabbit was nearly as big as me, and I had a hard time lifting it, but I soon discovered it was not only alive, but mean! Mean as hell, with awful sharp claws!

Now remember, this is early in the morning; I had just gotten out of bed. I had on only a T-shirt and underpants. It scratched me a dozen times on my belly and I actually bled. Everyone thought it was funny and had a great laugh, but I never went near that beast again.

Everyone else seemed to like the rabbit; they even named it Molly. Thinking back on it, I'm sure it ended up in a rabbit stew. If so, no one told me. I think I would have taken pleasure in that meal.

Jim kept his bunny caged and well fed all that summer. By the time winter was on us, Doc Sheen had convinced him it was time to leave the cage door open. The rabbit would be on his own, more or less, from that time on. Yet he hung around the Sheens' home for many years. He had a snug bed out of the weather in his cage in the coal shed and an occasional carrot that somehow found its way into the cage.

The last time I used my pet box before it became kindling wood was when my brother, Gibby, got a job with Smith Construction Company the summer before his senior year in high school. Smith had the contract to remove the rails of the abandoned Denver & Rio Grande Railroad spur between Park City and the cement plant in Parley's Canyon. Hal Himes, a good friend of Gibby, told me years later that the crew was composed of an Indian, former section hands, town drunks, but mostly high school kids.

Gibby's job turned into a source for a new type of pet. When they reached the lower part of Parley's Canyon, he brought me a horntoad lizard in his lunch box.

Horntoads are strange creatures and I probably had the only one in Park City. Counting the tail, they are about five inches long and almost three inches wide and, as their name implies, they are covered with horns. In reality, they are small spikes about a half inch long all over their backs.

Gibby told me that if a snake swallowed one whole, the horntoad would just rub the inside of the snake's belly until the snake got real sick and swelled up and burst open. Then the horntoad would just walk away like nothing had happened.

Well, I begged him and begged him to catch a snake and bring it home so we could witness this wonderful thing. But Gibby said the only snakes that they had encountered were rattlesnakes and Mom would get mad if he brought one of those home.

The horntoad lived in my pet box for about three days before it up and disappeared. Gibby brought home a second one and it, too, disappeared. Then a third, and the same thing happened. I went over my box with a fine-tooth comb, searching for the crack, or the secret trap door, or whatever means they used for escape, but all to no avail. I gave up on being the proud owner of a horntoad. Years later I became convinced that Dad was the one who had released them. He probably thought I was too young and dumb to care for one.

Gibby's job helping remove the rails and ties for the Denver & Rio Grande Railroad was not his introduction to hard work. Throughout his teen years he found all sorts of employment, such as picking fruit in and around Orem, Utah, and helping his friend Tom Hoover deliver groceries for Tom's father at the Star Meat and Grocery store.

One time, for some reason or other, he took me along, probably because Mom had to go shopping or on some other errand. That day one of their deliveries was to Bessie, the owner of one of Park City's houses of ill repute. It was their last delivery of the day; I guess they hoped to be invited in or something.

They left me in the truck while they carried in several paper bags of groceries. They were gone only three or four minutes, but when they returned they were both excited. They were laughing and talking all at the same time.

I couldn't understand or follow their conversation. I know they were talking about clothes, long hair and long legs, plus getting a good tip for delivering the groceries, and a bunch of stuff I couldn't understand.

When we got home, I wanted to tell Mom all about the day with the "big kids." But Gibby kept interrupting. He even let me help him bring in the coal and kindling that night. Soon I found other things to do with my time. Unfortunately, that was the only time I got to deliver groceries with Gibby and Tom.

Gibby also worked baling hay for various farms in the Snyderville Basin area. Once he came home with what was called a "bastard lamb" as payment for several days of work on Bitner's farm.

A bastard lamb is one that the mother sheep rejects for some unknown reason. If the lamb isn't hand fed, it soon dies. I'm still debating whether giving Gibby that lamb was an act of compassion or a cheap way to pay off a naïve teenage kid.

I think the lamb was the neatest pet a family could have. It was not long without a name. I bet everyone who gets a female lamb names her Mary. It's not original, but it's fitting.

Mary was fun. Any kid with any feelings at all would take delight in bottle-feeding a baby lamb. She needed and got attention from the whole family. If it was the least bit cold outside, some member of the family would let her in.

A lamb on a linoleum floor is something to behold. Here's an animal noted for its firm footing on almost all terrain, but on a slick linoleum floor it's akin to watching W.C. Fields dressed in a tutu dancing the Nutcracker Ballet. Her legs could do splits in four different directions at the same time.

As in the nursery rhyme, Mary wanted to follow you wherever you went. I remember Gibby saying how hard it was to explain to City Marshal Chuck Thomas why he had a lamb in the Post Office on Main Street.

The purpose of keeping the lamb was to fatten her up during the summer so we could enjoy the meat she would provide the coming winter. Well, the best-made plans sometimes don't work as intended. It seemed that everyone in the family lost their taste for lamb.

Dad knew we could not keep her through the winter; we lacked both the housing and the knowledge to do her justice. Sometime in mid-September we loaded Mary into the backseat of dad's old Studebaker and made our way to George Condas's sheep ranch. Condas agreed to take the lamb and actually gave Gibby five dollars for her.

I couldn't understand why we had to give her up. It took me years to acknowledge that Dad did the right thing. It was probably harder on him than anyone else, having to play the "heavy" in finding a new home for Mary.

I cried as we drove away. Mary was at the fence making fearful cries that, even today, if I close my eyes and listen, I can still hear.

Winter in Old Park City

The Silver King Coalition Building towers over the surrounding structures in this winter scene looking northeast from the front porch of the Kimball home on Woodside Avenue. *Photo courtesy of the Kimball Archive.*

Watching fancy-dressed skiers with their expensive equipment whiz past my house on their way to the Town Lift leaves me a little envious, yet triggers memories of winters in the Park City of my youth.

Winters during the 1940s and '50s were hard. Filling coal buckets each night after school became an unending task that generations of Park City kids don't fondly remember.

Parlor stoves and the kitchen range were the only source of heat for most homes. A water jacket that ran through the kitchen range heated water that was stored in a tank in the bathroom, but there was seldom enough for a real hot bath. Baths were a Friday night affair; Mom would heat a couple of pans of hot water on the stove to aid the hot-water tank in filling the bathtub.

Nearly all homes were heated with coal. The type of coal indicated the wealth of one's family. Gauged, washed and oiled slack that was mined in Price, Utah, or Rock Springs, Wyoming, was premium. On the other end of the scale was Coalville lump coal.

Coalville coal had a high sulfur content, making eyes water and giving clothes the odor of a burnt match. We used the blunt end of an ax to break it up so that it would fit into the stove.

Occasionally, a neighborhood would be plagued by a coal thief. There was a man named Mitchell who lived up the street from us in an apartment house managed by Oscar Clegg. Early one winter, Oscar discovered that his coal pile was vanishing faster than usual. On the other hand, Mitchell's shed was always empty. (Each apartment in a common building has an individual coal shed.)

Oscar solved the problem by putting a lock on his own shed, and other renters soon followed suit. It was not long before Mitchell moved. Unfortunately for us, he rented the old McDonough house next to ours.

Mitchell must not have been too bright. Even I could figure it out: footsteps in the newly fallen snow leading from a bedroom window in his home to our coal shed, then back again.

The hardware store did a booming business that winter selling padlocks, and Mitchell became superb specimen of physical conditioning as he roamed farther afield and lugged home buckets of ill-gotten coal, dogs snapping at his heels. Most people enjoyed his performance, each wondering with some delight as to who would be his next victim. It added a diversion to an otherwise dull winter. And we all wondered what action, if any, the police marshal would take since he was, coincidentally, Mitchell's father-in-law.

One year, when John L. Lewis's coal-miners' union (United Mine Workers of America) went on strike, it caught many families unprepared. Most would order their winter supply of coal in autumn, ensuring that the coal shed would be filled to capacity for the coming winter. But my family was caught unprepared with a short supply of coal when the strike dried up the market. I was delighted, however, to go with my brothers, gunnysack in hand, searching for any lost coal scattered along the town railroad tracks. (This pleased me greatly because, like many younger siblings, I was often shunned.)

One cold Sunday evening we were huddled around the parlor stove kept alight with some old broken-up wood furniture and listening to the radio. Bob Hope was ending his show with his theme song, "Thanks for the Memories." At time he would ad-lib the lyrics to fit the political situation at hand. That night he sang something to the effect of, "We give thanks for the furniture we're burning tonight." My family laughed so hard they had tears in their eyes. I missed the joke and no one would explain it to me.

I loved that stove. In the evening we would all sit around it doing various chores: Paul and I doing homework, Dad reading the newspaper, and Mom either reading or mending clothes. I loved to take off my wet shoes, place my feet on the stove, and watch the steam roll off my wet stockings. Occasionally I would get into trouble because I could not resist the temptation of melting a crayon on the stove. The stench of paraffin could not be hidden and I was always caught. Mom had a good nose.

Often, in the dark, we listened to the radio, usually some thriller such as "Inner Sanctum Mysteries," sponsored by Sanka decaffeinated coffee, or "Suspense!" which was sponsored by Autolite sparkplugs. The stove's dancing orange flames glowed through the isinglass windows, which, together with the occasional crackling and popping of the coal, gave the room a warm but eerie feeling.

The family coal shed crowned with snow during the winter of 1951-52. *Photo courtesy of the Kimball Archive.*

(Isinglass is a mineral in the mica family which, when split into thin sheets, is transparent. It was used in stoves instead of glass.)

Central heating has relegated the fireplace to a show item. It's pretty, but it's nothing to build a childhood around. When you had to buck snowdrifts three feet high to make your way to the coal shed and lug back two buckets of coal, each weighing 25 pounds, an alliance between you and the stove slowly developed.

Keeping the coal buckets full was our job. My oldest brother, Gibby, had the duty until Paul was old enough. Then, sometime around age twelve, the duty fell to me. Before that I was in charge of bringing in the kindling; both were never-ending chores.

One drawback to the stove was that the fire would burn out at night. Not many people today have the privilege of being greeted each morning by the sight of their own breath. Dad would get up around 6 a.m. and "shake down" the grates of the kitchen range. Then he would make a bed of wadded-up newspaper, followed by kindling wood, and on top of that some lump coal. Soon a roaring fire would turn the stovepipe cherry red. He would also build a fire in the parlor stove before he left for work.

But it took time to heat the old house. I hated getting out of bed. The floors were so cold they burned your feet. I'd make a dash to the space behind the kitchen range to dress. I always wore long johns and two pairs of stockings, so dressing was a difficult chore.

Before the end of Word War II, Main Street and Park Avenue were the only streets that were regularly plowed, and cars were seldom driven in the winter months. All cars in those days were rear-wheel-drive and lacked the weight, power and traction to get around on the back streets.

At times it could be weeks before the back streets got plowed. The traffic on these streets was somewhat restricted to garbage pickup and coal- and grocery-delivery trucks. (All the grocery stores had home delivery, usually on Saturdays.) All these trucks had snow tires and were chained up for greater traction.

Some of these back streets were turned into coasting lanes for sledding. The city apparently had some sort of rotating system for these lanes because the designated streets seemed to change from year to year. Fortunately, Woodside Avenue in front of our house was one of the lanes. You could start at the top of Woodside and, if lucky, coast all the way to the high school (now the Park City Library).

At times we formed "ramming parties" and tried to upset one another. Many a boy imagined himself in the cockpit of a Spitfire, the enemy swarming all around.

The bond one had with his sled seemed like an extension of oneself. We each believed we had the best sled in town, regardless of what others would say. The older boys thought of sledding as a way to get close to some girl. They were always giggling and screaming, whispering and hugging, and missing all the real fun.

The noise that a sled made was slight, but it was a unique sound that I have not heard for years. At night you could hear a sled speeding down the street and a "clink" when it hit some grit or sand. You could follow its progress by the sparks that flew.

There was some risk in coasting. Every year a half dozen or so kids would end up with broken bones. I can even recall two deaths, both when sledding children were hit by cars.

My father owned a toboggan. However, after many years of broken bones, the last of which belonged to a dear friend of my mother's, Dad took an ax to the toboggan. I'm still sulking because

The author in 1949 between ramparts of snow in front of the family home.
Photo courtesy of the Kimball Archive.

I never got a chance to solo on that thing, but we certainly had a very nice fire that night.

Sledding was by far the most popular winter sport, but most kids also tried their hand at skiing, and a few were quite good. The skis we used were primitive by today's standards. Skis were wood, usually maple, and, when new, each came with a leather foot strap. We would take a rubber strip cut from a car tire inner tube, slip one end over the front of the shoe and the other end over the heel of the shoe. For lightweight young kids, it worked well.

Most kids didn't have ski poles and the majority of us thought poles were for sissies. Kids who can't afford stuff often use that word to describe those who can. Besides, poles were of no use in ski jumping, and that is what most of us did.

Once there was a great wooden ski jump built on the hillside just south of the first Creole Mine dump. For years ski jumping events were held here, and old-timers often talked about the time that the Pathé News (movie newsreels) featured the ski tournament held there in March 1927.

The jump had collapsed a few years before we started skiing. Each winter we pledged to rebuild this onetime famous jump come the following summer, but each summer there were better things to do.

The ski jump in my neighborhood was built out of snow on the "Old Back Road" (the extension of Norfolk Avenue, which was platted but never constructed due to avalanche and snow-slide danger). We would build a jump two or three feet high and jump it over and over again – which, in time, became quite boring, but all in all served its purpose in teaching the basics of skiing.

I can recall only one injury happening on this jump: a broken ankle. That year Eddy Berry had received new skis with fancy bindings, ski boots, and a set of ski poles. The early ski bindings were called bear-trap bindings because they did not release the foot from the ski and broken ankles were common. Yet every one of us wanted a pair.

I finally inherited one of my brothers' sets of skis that had the bindings on them, but I didn't have ski boots that would work with the bindings. Fortunately there was a cobbler shop on Main Street and he did a land-office business modifying regular boots

A tobogganist shows off his version of "keeping your tips up." Some of the unplowed back streets such as Woodside Avenue were turned into coasting lanes for sledding. *Photo courtesy of the Kimball Archive.*

or winter shoes to work as ski boots. He would add nearly an inch of hard rubber to the back heel and then cut a deep grove around the edge so the binder cable would fit snugly. The boots worked great, and as often as not during a serious spill the heel of the boot would rip off before the ankle snapped. Still, the skier with the missing heel would curse the cobbler for doing a poor job on his boots.

From the late 1940s onward, the Snow Park ski resort in Deer Valley, owned by Otto Carpenter and Bob Burns, ran a successful operation. They had a homemade single-seat ski lift. The towers were made of pines cut from the ski runs. The chairs were attached to used cable from the local mines, and the power source was, if I remember right, an old Model A Ford engine. The whole operation was held together with sweat and love.

Riding the lifts was an experience in itself. Between lift towers your skis were often on the ground. Then, as you approached a

The Snow Park ski area, built by Otto Carpenter and Bob Burns in Deer Valley.
Courtesy of the Bea Kummer Collection, Park City Museum.

tower, you would suddenly lift off the ground. But it would not be long until your skis were back in the grooves of previous lift riders.

I, and most of my friends, often could not afford the price of a lift pass. But usually, after a snowstorm, Otto would offer you a half-day pass if you and your friends would mount your skis and sidestep up the hillside. We all considered it was a great bargain.

It would take us all morning to cover an area smaller than a football field. We were packing runs that today a snow-grooming machine could do in one pass.

During one summer, my friends and I hiked up on the hill to watch Otto cutting down trees for his ski runs. Each time a tree began to fall, Otto would call out, "Timber!" and then sing at the top of his lungs, "The timber wolf calls 'timber' – when he sees a pretty girl." We all though he was great, and a good singer.

I knew Otto quite well. He and my father, both carpenters, often worked on the same jobs in Salt Lake and rode down together. Then, in 1950-51, they both accepted jobs helping build a nickel mill on the island of New Caledonia, a French possession in the South Pacific. The builders were the same people who owned and operated the local Pacific Bridge mill that was located below town in an area that is now known as Prospector Square.

Many years later, when I was the Farmers Insurance agent in Park City, I had Otto's cars and trailers insured. Later, I took a job with him repairing a few senior citizens' homes at Summit County's expense.

A few years after Otto's death in October 1996, I was a member of the Park City Historic Preservation Board. The Carpenter family was in the process of selling their parents' home at 1021 Norfolk Avenue and surrounding land. The property would bring in more money if it were free of structures.

I fought hard to prevent Otto Carpenter's home from being demolished. There was nothing special about the house. At that time it was relatively new (he built it in 1942). However, I did not want to be associated with the destruction of the home of a pioneer in the Park City ski industry and argued that it was worth saving.

I'm sad to say that many hard feeling were caused in this matter. The house was saved, but today, wedged between several new homes and finished with the same type of trim and paint, it is hard to find in the maze. And there is no placard or any other way to recognize it.

On a sad note, Bob Burns, Carpenter's partner in Snow Park, suffered a tragic death when an acetylene-welding tank exploded and his home burned in the fall of 1981.

Because of Park City's elevation and our primitive equipment to deal with the demands of winter, we had it much harder than most of the rest of the state. In hindsight, I am convinced that our winters and mountaintop living gave us pride in our lifestyle.

I remember Danny Wright, an upperclassman, coming to school one day with a bad limp. When asked if he had been in some sort of accident, he looked puzzled and said, "Accident? No accident. I'm a ridge-runner. One leg is a little longer than the other. Get me on a ridge and I don't limp. I can walk or run faster than any flatlander."

We took pride in our mountains and our snow. I remember a standard song we sang around the Marsac School during the winter. It was sung to the tune of "When It's Springtime in the Rockies" and went like this: "When it's springtime in Park City and ninety nine below, all the kids go swimming in fifty feet of snow."

During the savage winter of 1950-51, the Utah National Guard was called in to clear the streets of the heavy white stuff. The huge rotary snowplows filled many vacant lots two stories high, or more, with snow.

I don't know how much snow fell that year. The west side of our house that faces Treasure Mountain was covered with snow. You had to turn on the lights to see in the back bedroom and the kitchen. Keeping a path open to the coal shed was near impossible.

It was really tough at our house because my brother Gibby had joined the Navy and was gone. Dad had taken the construction job in New Caledonia, so neither was around to help.

The shoveling to the coal shed and keeping the fires going was up to my brother Paul and me. At one time the snow became so deep that the bottom of the staircase leading to our house became a tunnel.

Mom noticed some Steller's jays and started putting out breadcrumbs for them on the landing leading to coal shed. There we witnessed something we thought delightful but in reality was a struggle to survive. A cottontail rabbit showed up and tried to horn in on the feeding birds. They wanted nothing to do with him. They fluttered their wings, screamed and pecked at him; it looked as though he would go without any crumbs. He paused, studied the situation, then dropped his head and charged as if he were a raging bull, butting birds left and right until he had cleared a place in the middle of the scattered breadcrumbs. He feasted until full, then retreated from the screaming birds.

Earning money in the winter was a challenge, but if you were diligent and the snow was heavy, you could always find someone willing to pay you to shovel it. Mary Shields, a nurse at the Miners Hospital, owned a house just south of the Mormon First Ward building (now known as The Blue Church Lodge.) Mary's house was at street level on Park Avenue, but the back of the house faced east and the hillside was steep; her backyard was at least 16 feet lower than the street. The house had a pyramid roof and an ice dam would build up over a foot thick running nearly around the entire edge of the roof.

That winter she hired Bobby Clegg and me to shovel her roof. Besides the ice dam, there was at least four to five feet of snow covering the structure. The snow was easy to remove just by cutting it into blocks small enough to handle and giving it a shove. It would slide off, sailing into the yard.

The ice was a different matter. Shovels could not even dent it. I finally got hold of an ax and began to chop away. It worked well where sunlight was reaching the roof and the temperature was a little warmer, but on the east side of the roof, where the sun had passed and it was in the shade, the ice was frozen solid.

I chopped and chopped and was about to give up when the whole thing gave way. I was standing on the ice and, along with the ice, took flight. The roof at this point was about 26 feet higher than the ground.

It's a thrilling experience sailing through the air. Fortunately there was an apple tree that helped break my fall; tree limbs and branches flew in all directions. I landed in good shape and, without giving it much thought, proclaimed it a new sport.

We took turns jumping off the roof but had to quit when the apple tree began to look a little shabby. If we were smart, I bet we could have charged Mary for pruning her tree. But back in those days we didn't know about such things.

We recruited nearly all our friends to try out our new sport. First we used Drapers' garage, located about 498 Woodside Avenue. It sat just south of the stairs where Fifth Street would have been if there had been a street. The jump from the roof of the garage to the ground below was a good 40 feet! It was great fun.

The deep snow began to pack tighter with each jump. We were thinking about quitting until some adults started shouting at us to get off the roof before one of us broke his neck. So, of course, that triggered one more jump. Then we were forced to listen while they lectured us about all the dangers we faced by jumping.

To us, the dangers were obvious. That's why we were doing it!

We finally found a location where we were free of harassment: the Silver King aerial tramway. The third tower up from the Coalition Building was far enough up the mountain that we didn't care if anyone was watching. And, as far as anyone showing up to stop us, well, people in general are lazy, especially facing a hard walk in deep snow. We felt safe.

We jumped, and each time we climbed higher up the tower until we were nearly 50 feet off the ground. No one got hurt, and I guess we got it out of our system, because it was the only winter I recall that snow jumping was popular with my group.

Parades, Fireworks and Homemade Root Beer

Cub Scouts struggle with flags in a Park City Fourth of July Parade.
Photo courtesy of the Kendall Webb Collection, Park City Museum.

Springtime is something that people talk about in Park City, but it really is more of a fanciful thing than a season. Some of the newcomers used to call it mud season, and for a time that term was accurate. But now all the streets are blacktop and it's harder to find mud. I suppose the hiking and bike trails in the mountains are still muddy in the springtime. But since it's against my nature to go in search of mud, I wouldn't know. In my childhood, what spring we got was short; winter always resented giving up and would not leave without a fight. Just when the cherry trees were in full bloom, that last snowstorm, often as not, would rage through. Garden-wise no one felt safe until after Memorial Day. We all loved May because it led to our summer break.

June is the grandest month of the year. The greens are greener, all the flowers are brighter and the birds sing a sweeter song. In adolescence you never look back, only ahead. Summer meant fishing, picnics, hiking, biking, trading comic books and making homemade root beer.

Each summer Dad would supervise us in making a huge batch of root beer. It was a family affair. We would search for soda-pop bottles and beer bottles to fill. I would curse myself for all the bottles that I had already redeemed for a penny apiece. Finally, though, we would have enough.

We would clean and then boil the bottles to make sure they were sanitized. Then, in a huge crock, we would dump sugar, Hires root-beer extract and a little yeast, and add cold water; then we'd mix it, fill the bottles and cap them with Bulldog bottle caps. Then the bottles would have to be placed on their sides in a warm place to age. After six days or so they would be ready to drink.

In our case, we usually left it until a bottle exploded. You really knew it was ready when that happened. If the bottles were placed upright in a cool place, the root beer would keep for months. Usually, it was consumed in one or two weeks.

On hot summer days, when it was too hot to play, we would sit in the shade on the front porch sipping ice-cold root beer and reading comic books. They were better than any school primer. Trading comic books was even more fun than reading them.

My buddy Raymond and I were in a sort of competition when it came to trading comic books. We did what we called snugging. We both claimed to be the best at snugging. Stealing is the right word, but who would want to label themselves as thieves? So we snugged. In the midst of a trade, we would slip a second comic book inside the one we were trading for. We would start out with five or six books and come home with ten or more.

Some of the people we traded with were adults. Stella Duke, who was in her late thirties, loved comic books, but most of hers were romance stories. It did not matter. Her books were in mint condition, and we would trade them to Evelyn Hill or some other girl.

Snugging was not confined to us alone. In one trade with Jimmy Hall, I snugged four books but my stack increased by only one. Raymond claimed he came away two short. He was so mad that he wanted us to confront Jimmy. But he was two years older than us, and he might possibly expose a tiny amount of guilt on our part. We'd get even the next time.

Summer evenings and nights were fun. We would play pomp-pomp pull away, or kick-the-can. To choose who would be "it," we would get in a huddle and each person would secretly pick the make of an automobile. The person who was the last "it" in the game the evening before would name cars until he picked an auto that someone had chosen. That someone would become "it."

Since my middle name is Austin, for a long time I would choose the Austin car. Unfortunately, everyone knew it was my name. After a time, I got tired of being "it" and learned the names of a few more cars.

After it was too dark to play, we would sit on a lawn and talk. In those discussions I learned most of the facts of life, some factual, some ridiculous. I heard all the latest dirty jokes and laughed even when I didn't understand a thing.

Everyone looked forward to the Independence Day and Labor Day celebrations. They both followed the same format. The 21-gun salute always happened at the crack of dawn. Twenty-one charges of dynamite were set in place on top of Masonic Mount (now better known as the Aerie) and, usually just a little before 5 a.m., the earth-shattering booms started. There was always a pause of 15 to 60 seconds between charges. Windows would shake, dogs would bark and cats would hide under beds. It was a grand awakening for a wonderful day.

For years Mom would make me a new outfit for the Fourth of July, matching shirt and pants, out of a soft light-blue material. I felt special. On these holidays, I'd often receive as much as a dollar spending money.

We would all line up on the dock of the Union Pacific Depot, hundreds of kids of both sexes, all ages and various sizes. The floats would gather at the Silver Town Service Station (formerly the Kimball Service Station) at the corner of Heber and Park avenues.

The line of march would always be the same. First came the color guards – this duty falling to Park City's veterans from the most recent war – carrying the flag high. Then came city officials on Independence Day, union officials on Labor Day. After that

Kids hang from a fire truck in a Fourth of July Parade.
In the background is the Salt Lake House, which was demolished in 1969.
Photo courtesy of the Kendall Webb Collection, Park City Museum.

were the fire engines, always carrying the children of key members of the volunteer fire department. Then, of course, there were the bands – first the Marsac School band and later the Park City High School marching band.

Intermingled throughout the parade were the floats, all made locally by home talent. The parades were for the people of Park City and no one gave a thought about any outlanders who might be present. Bringing up the tail end of the parade were the kids. We marched with pride and, for the most part, kept in good order.

The route was from the foot of Main Street and Heber Avenue up Main Street all the way to the top. At the turn-around, volunteers and union officials would pass out a dime to each child. If you were quick and knew what you were doing, like Raymond, you could come away with two or three dimes.

The parade would then head back down Main Street and disband at the War Memorial Building (now the home of Park City Live). Here some of the local politicians would give patriotic speeches at a podium erected in front of the building. Then kids' foot races and the soapbox derby would be held on Main Street. A coin scramble (coins of various denominations hidden in sawdust) would be held just north of the Post Office.

The drilling and mucking-machine contests were usually held behind the City Hall (now the home of the Park City Museum). The saloons and taverns were filled three-deep at the bar, and Pop Jenks Confectionery and the Central Drug Store were crowded with kids. In the afternoon there was always a free movie consisting of shorts, comedy shows and cartoons. It was a full day.

As for fireworks, it seemed everyone supplied their own. There were the legal fireworks such as sparklers, snakes and a few other items. Outlawed items such as firecrackers and rockets were easy to come by, if you had the money. We who were without that kind of money took pride in building our own.

Carbide was common in Park City because it was used in the miners' lamps; every family seemed to have some. If you placed a little carbide in a fruit jar, added a little water and put the lid on tight, it was just a matter of time until it exploded with a boom, sending glass flying in all directions. We were always impatient with the wait and would throw rocks at the bottle; it's a wonder that no one was ever injured.

Another type of improvised bomb involved taking two large bolts and a nut one-half inch in size or larger, cutting the heads off a handful of wooden matches and placing them in the nut, and screwing the bolts down on both ends of the nut until they were snug. Then we would throw this device up in the air. When it hit a hard surface it would usually explode, making a grand noise.

In my neighborhood after dark, Jimmy Jennings' grandfather, Doc Sheen, would direct Jimmy and his sister Freddie in lighting all kinds of fireworks at the intersection of Norfolk Avenue and the Crescent Tramway. It was a fun evening. A few years later the public dances would take up my evenings.

I'm sure there were wildfires in and around Park City that were started by fireworks, but to be honest I can't think of one. I do know of one fire that I was directly involved with. I was helping Bob Cullen and my brother Paul build a big skyscraper structure out of those wooden boxes that strawberries used to be sold in. We were just behind the Tarzan Tree, located just to the south of the Sheens' property.

These boxes were great to build castles or other structures with and then burn them down. The flames would dance high for a few moments, then die down and burn out in just a few minutes. I had seen older kids do this once or twice a little way up the Tramway, just behind the Wilson house, and I was excited to help in actually burning one.

Well, I guess the grass and brush around the box skyscraper were extremely dry; before anyone realized it, the mountainside was on fire. Bob and Paul were throwing dirt at the fire and trying to kick it out, all to no avail. Paul screamed at me to go home and get a bucket of water. I didn't need to be told twice.

I raced home, but my five-year-old brain had formed a better idea. I turned on the water to the tub and announced that I was going to take a bath. I was half-undressed before Mom asked me what was going on. She knew something was wrong. It wasn't Friday and, even then, I never volunteered to take my bath. But before she could question me, the curfew whistle at City Hall started blowing: two long calls signaled a fire. Then the siren of the fire truck could be heard wailing. Mom, smelling smoke, stepped out onto the back porch to look around.

By the time she returned I was naked and in the tub, and just beginning to feel safe. I had seen many crime movies, and heard many detective shows on the radio, and knew that the police never arrested naked people who were taking a bath. It was a safe bet to take a bath when the police might be involved.

The fire department put the fire out in short order and the Tarzan Tree wasn't damaged. Paul and Bob were in serious trouble with their parents. And the best part? I was hardly in any trouble at all. Both Paul and Bob were a little mad because I didn't come back with a bucket of water, but that was soon forgotten.

The Tarzan Tree was a wonderful place. It was squeezed in between the Sheens' property and the Silver King aerial tramway. Long before Edgar Rice Burroughs created the character of Tarzan, generations of Park City youths dating back to the 1890s played here, swinging from ropes or building tree houses, every generation claiming it as their own.

I got to see my first and only compound fracture here. Bibs (William) Hewitson took a wicked fall while swinging from a rope. As he got up, you could see the bone protruding from his arm. I still remember the sober look on his face as he started for home, repeating to himself, over and over again, "No use crying about it." God, I thought he was tough.

In the autumn, this giant maple would turn the most brilliant shades of red, bringing joy to all who beheld it. Unfortunately, progress is paramount: it was cut down in the 1980s to make way for the Old Town ski lift.

Bob's Army

Bob Mawhinney in 1951 in his Eagle Scout uniform.
He earned the rank of Eagle Scout at the tender age of 12.
Photo courtesy of the Kendall Webb Collection, Park City Museum.

One of my all-time friends is Bob Mawhinney. We go back farther than either of us can remember. He is what you would describe as a doer. He is not one to sit back if there a problem that needs to be fixed. He gets busy and finds a solution. It might not be the right fix, but it was always good enough for me.

He probably liked girls before most of us. I remember once – I think it was during the second grade – that Bob studied all the girls in our class and asked me to do the same. I looked them over, but they all seemed about the same. After all, they were girls. But

Bob proclaimed that the girl who always seemed to wear the longest stockings was undoubtedly the prettiest in our class. That was Nancy Gibbons. She always wore stockings of various colors that went above her knees. I agreed with Bob. If he thought she was pretty, then I guess she was.

In school you were forced to be around girls, but I tried to keep out of their way. That was my rule since the first grade. Back then I thought the difference between boys and girls was like the difference between dogs (boys) and cats (girls), and that boys were stronger and tougher than girls. Fortunately, Peggy Marcellin, a farm girl from Snyderville, corrected this uninformed notion of mine by knocking me down and pinning me during recess two days in a row.

But Bob was a neat kid and, if you want to play with neat kids, it's often a good idea to go along with their judgment. I'd go along with any ideas he had about girls, just as long as he didn't want me to fight any of them. And you know what? A few years later I could see that Bob was right all along.

Bob had an aunt who really liked him and accepted his friends with open arms. His aunt Clara (Clara Roberta Mawhinney, June 24, 1894 – April 7, 1957) owned a large boardinghouse at 163 Heber Avenue. Clara lived in a neat apartment upstairs in the back of the house and rented out the rest. Altogether, I think there were four apartments. There was a long boardwalk that stretched all the way to Main Street. She owned several outbuildings, comprised of old coal sheds and a barn that more recently served as car garages – when renters had cars, that is.

Poison Ditch (Silver Creek) was somewhat underground here; upstream, several of the large capstones covering the creek had been removed to unplug stoppages. As the saying went, "Keep it flowing, Coalville needs the water."

A little upstream and on the east side was the Star Meat & Grocery slaughterhouse. It was no longer in use, but made a neat place to play around. All in all, it was a great place to play, plot and dream.

Bob liked secrets and he could really keep them. A while back he told me about one secret he had kept for more than 40 years.

He once won a fancy bow-and-arrow set at the Annual Bazaar held at the War Memorial Building. It was a real hunting set: the arrow points were razor sharp and flared out in four fins.

The next day in his aunt's backyard, he decided to see how far he could shoot an arrow into the air. It went really high and came down all the way over on Main Street – right through the roof of Fonce Martinez's Model A Ford Coupe parked in front of the Cozy Saloon. It was embedded in the driver's seat, really deep. Bob crept

Bob's aunt, Clara Mawhinney, owned this boardinghouse at 163 Heber Avenue that included a small apartment she let the boys use as a clubhouse. *Photo courtesy of the Himes-Buck Digital Collection, Park City Museum.*

over to the car and, when the coast was clear, opened the driver's door, extracted the arrow and made his escape.

Now Fonce had the reputation of being one of the meanest, toughest miners who ever lived in Park City, and to Bob's credit – he was real smart that way – he decided not to share this secret with anyone. And even though Fonce has been dead for a number of years, it was only recently that he declassified the Bow-Shooting Incident to the general public, or at least to his friends.

It was at Clara's that Bob decided we should recruit a secret army to fight Russian kids when World War III broke out. He was convinced that the Commies would send kids over here to fight us when they discovered we American kids were fighting them.

It made perfect sense to me, and I became committed! It was bad enough that the U.S. Government had stolen our idea to build a bomb that could destroy a city, and now those stinking Reds in Russia had built one too! It was just too much. I told Bob I was ready for the fight and to sign me up.

Fortunately for us, times were tough in the apartment-rental business, and Clara had a small unit she let us use as a clubhouse. It was a midsize room with a sink and stove, and even had an attached bathroom. It really made a neat clubhouse.

Somewhere along the way, most of us started calling her "Aunt Clara," and I don't think it bothered her any; she was that kind of person.

Sometimes, when I was walking uptown from home, she would call me over and ask if I would take a letter to the Post Office. Often she would ask me to stop at Mrs. Maude McPhee's storefront house on Main Street to pick up a letter to be mailed.

Mrs. McPhee was an elderly widow lady who always seemed to be dressed in a housecoat. She would spend hours looking out her windows at the doings on Main Street. Rumor was that she was looking for her son who the family had disowned for his drinking and gambling many years earlier. I heard her husband had operated a cigar factory in the building.

Mrs. McPhee often gave me a nickel tip, and once in a while it would be a dime. My mother had told me to not accept tips from widows. "It's just not done," she said. So I'd always tell her "No thanks" as I held my hand out to receive the reward. It was one of my friends who told me that I was putting my hand out before I said no. You know, an eleven- or twelve-year-old can be embarrassed. I tried to keep my hand in check after that, but the greed for that candy money was always faster than my mouth.

Bob followed the Cold War with great interest and concern. He was convinced the Soviet Union (Russia) would soon invade America, so he made plans for his secret kids' army.

He based his ranking system somewhat along the lines of the Boy Scouts. In Scouting, the ranking starts with Tenderfoot and advances as follows: Second Class, First, Star, Life and Eagle. Bob cleverly changed the names of the ranks and invented a few merit badges that the members of his army needed to pass to be promoted. I don't remember our rankings for sure, but it was something similar to Half Moon, Half Moon with a Star, Full Moon and the Sun.

The best part of his army was that he made me second-in-command. Come to think of it, that probably is the highest and grandest thing I have ever achieved in life.

Of course, all armies need funding. Dues of 15 cents a week for each member were imposed. The organization worked great except for that bit about paying dues. Only one or two members ever paid the full amount. A few paid part of the amount and claimed that is all they had. The rest claimed they were broke, yet we would see them at the movies every Friday night. If questioned, the standard reply was, "Mom gave me money for the movies but nothing else." That was pretty much my own story, so I guess they were telling the truth.

One of the merit badges Bob insisted on was the Dog Badge. Bob had a new dog that he named Spot. He thought it was fitting that we should know the breeds of different dogs. Other than a few pictures of different breeds we could find in magazines, it was a difficult job. I don't think anyone in Park City owned what they called pedigree dogs. Maybe the brown bird dogs that belonged to Hugh Steele (the owner of The Cozy), but that was about it. I think Bob was using us to find out what breed Spot was.

Other important things included expertise with a slingshot – or what we called a "flipper crutch" – and rock throwing. We did collect enough money for Bob to buy a few knives when he was in Salt Lake City visiting his dentist. Bob actually would go to Salt Lake City on the Lewis Brothers Stage Line all by himself, and he knew his way around the downtown business district. I think all of us were impressed.

He purchased the knives in a war-surplus store. One was the most wicked knife I have ever seen. It was a long-bladed thing, made for killing, and we all knew that if any adults discovered we had it, they would confiscate it. So to this day it remains buried in our first mountain hideout 100 yards uphill from the second Creole Mine tailings dump.

The other knives were throwing knives. We placed a target on the side of Clara's barn and practice was mandatory for each member of the army.

We also built some military fortifications just west of the Denver & Rio Grande Railroad spur line that ran up through Deer Valley. Our foxholes were quite close to Bessie's whorehouse. We all seemed to know what went on there but were too young to care. Besides, when the fighting started, they would be thankful for our protection. It was a shame that our abilities were not up to our dreams. Our secret hideout was never completed; truth is, we hardly got started on it.

One cold stormy day we were all in the room that Aunt Clara let us use as a clubhouse. She built a fire in the kitchen range to keep us warm, then retreated upstairs, probably to listen to soap operas on the radio, or whatever older people did for fun.

After the club had its official meeting, I started work on a secret project. I was going to make a bomb. I was confident I could build one; I had listened to older kids describe giant firecrackers that they had made. I just knew I could do as well or better than they could.

I had three 12-gauge shotgun shells that I borrowed from my brother Gibby. Using one of the throwing knives, I pried open the shells and removed the pellets, the wadding and the smokeless gunpowder. Thinking the empty shell casings were harmless – all I could see was the brass bases and the paper tubes – I tossed them into the kitchen range. I thought a good way to get rid of all traces of my work was by burning the evidence. I did not realize that those shells were still armed with primers.

It was about 90 seconds until all hell broke loose. **BROOM!** All four of the stove lids popped five feet or more straight up in the air and came crashing down with a clanking thud. The stove chimney had partly popped out from the wall and the room was filling with smoke.

Clara – well, it's remarkable how fast that old woman could come down those stairs. Grabbing a broom, she gave a swift smack to the chimney stack, driving it back into the brickwork. And in a jiffy she had all the stove lids back in place. Other than a little smoke, nothing seemed out of the ordinary.

After checking to see if we were all okay, all she had to say was, "Those damn coal miners must have left a blasting cap in the coal. I've a good mind to report them."

I gave up bomb-making that day. To be honest, it was kind of scary, but I still think I could have built a great bomb.

Keeping an army active is hard work. Most of our members were several years younger than Bob and me, and they just did not have the same grasp of the geopolitical problems we were living with that would lead us to war with the Soviet Union. And to be honest, I kinda thought they might be right in not wanting a war.

All these years later, I think that some of my funniest times, or the most interesting times as a child, were spent around Clara's place. From the first funeral I ever attended for a cat ... to digging up the same cat several weeks later to see if she had changed much. We used Clara's phone for prank calls, and when we really felt brave we would call girls.

Even as the army as an organization faded, other needs of the community would come into focus. And Bob, always the organizer, set things in motion. During the winter of 1950-51, when heavy snows threatened to close one of our favorite shortcuts – the one that cut diagonally through several vacant lots from Park Avenue, between Chuck Thomas's place and Maurine Foster's boardinghouse, to Main Street – Bob declared we'd keep it open. In a raging blizzard we would walk back and forth over the trail.

Bob named us the F.F.F. & H. (Feet, Foot, Fingers and Hand) Organization. He was good coming up with names. For weeks, every time it snowed we would get to work and were delighted at the number of people, including adults, who used our shortcut.

Fritch Garage

The Fritch Garage as it looked about 1950, before the fire.
Photo courtesy of the Kendall Webb Collection, Park City Museum.

In 1953, when school let out for the summer, I got a tip from my buddy Bob Mawhinney about a job opening for a service-station attendant at Fritch Garage. Bob could not take it since his family owned a competitor, Mawhinney Motor, a full-service garage combined with an Oldsmobile/Chevrolet automobile dealership. Fritch had the same setup except that he had the Dodge/Plymouth dealership.

It was my first real job. Before this my only means of making money was by shoveling steps and paths in the winter, and cutting grass in the summer, plus collecting beer and soda bottle to redeem for cash. One time, Raymond Beckstead and I had tried selling Christmas trees, but that didn't work out so well.

I should have said a Christmas tree – one tree. We cut down a beautiful five-footer up by the second Creole Mine dump. It didn't look quite so good by the time we got it off the mountain and lugged it around to prospective homes. We found that selling was a tougher job than logging, and our tree was beginning to leave a trail of pine needles behind.

We were about to give up hope of finding a buyer when we spied my sixth-grade teacher, Mrs. Paxton, returning home from shopping.

I was hesitant. She was far down on my list of favorite teachers, and I knew she disliked me. I remember someone telling me that she was born in South Africa. I placed South Africa just below Germany and Japan on my list of evil countries because of her.

With Ray's nudging, I asked, "Would you like to buy a Christmas tree?"

"How much?"

Ray and I had already decided that, if we could find a buyer, our minimum price would be 90 cents. They now charged us 45 cents each as adults at the show house.

"A dollar," I said.

She studied the tree for a moment and answered, "It isn't worth that much."

In unison we replied, "90 cents."

She reached into her bag, retrieved a coin purse and slowly dumped a handful of coins into my outstretched hand; a few fell to the ground.

Paxton lifted the tree out of Ray's hand and, with a bag of groceries in one hand and the tree in the other, climbed the flight of stairs to her house and was soon out of sight. We retrieved one nickel and three pennies off the frozen sidewalk and slowly counted our money – three times – and each time came up with the same amount: 72 cents. Paxton had cheated us out of 18 cents.

Raymond was outraged. "Go and tell her! We want all our money!"

"I ain't going."

"Why not? She's your teacher."

"That's why. I want to pass and get out of her class. If she flunks me, I'd die!"

"If you don't go, she will know how dumb you really are and flunk you."

Ray was a good arguer. But my fear of Mrs. Paxton was greater than his argument. She had thumped me on the back of my head a short time before the Christmas break, and I knew I couldn't win with her no matter which way I turned, so I stood my ground and challenged Ray to go. He then argued that he would have her next year and didn't want to get off to a bad start.

Ray's big sister Carol was always looking out for him and loaned us the 18 cents we needed for the movie, so things worked out. And I learned an important lesson. Some teachers really think some of their students are stupid. And I learned it's not good to trust anyone who has the power to make your life miserable. So I guess Mrs. Paxton was good at teaching me something.

The first day on a new job is terrifying. I would come to learn it doesn't matter if it's the first job or the last one; the first day is a bitch.

I was really out of my league at Fritch Garage. I was terrified I might be asked to drive a car. I had only driven my dad's '47 Oldsmobile and that was only to Snyderville to buy milk from Loertscher's dairy farm. And, of course, Dad was sitting next to me. Also, the Olds had a Hydromatic transmission, which meant there were no gears to shift, except reverse.

I asked Dad what to expect. He shrugged his shoulders and slowly said, "Just do what they tell you to do and you'll be okay." That wasn't much help, especially coming from a man who used to own his own service station.

Mom was more practical. She taught me how to count change back to the customer. Say a customer purchased an air gauge for

$1.39 and handed you a five-dollar bill. You would count the amount as you gave him back his change. You would start with "$1.39," then hand him a penny, "forty," then a dime, "fifty," then two quarters, "two dollars," then count out three more dollar bills. I practiced this for several hours with different combinations. Today, all that has changed with automation. Clerks do not know how to count out change, and hard currency itself may soon vanish.

Mom also lectured me on being courteous: "Always address a lady as 'ma' and a man as 'sir'. And keep busy. When times are slow, sweep the floor or wash the windows, and be sure to take out the trash."

She was right on all counts, but at the time I thought that she didn't know a damn thing about garages.

The service station where I started was not really Fritch's. Several months earlier, in the dead of winter, his garage had burned nearly to the ground. He thought he was out of business for good, but the community came to his rescue, holding public dances and other fundraisers, while many volunteered to rebuild his business. Park City was a great place back then.

While everybody was working on rebuilding Fritch's Garage, Johnny set up shop in a temporary location known locally as Horan's Station, located at 1260 Park Avenue, the next building north of Mawhinney Motor. The 1950s were hard in Park City, and Larry Horan had been forced to close the business not long after taking it over from his older brother Russ, who had accepted the job of manager of the Park City branch of First Security Bank.

At first, my job was to keep the temporary station open for the gas and oil trade. By early December, I would be at the real Fritch Garage.

I really felt stupid. I knew about the fire, but that's about all I knew. It was an eye-opener. I read the comic stripe Gasoline Alley

The Fritch Garage as it looked after the community banded together to rebuild it.
Photo courtesy of the Himes-Buck Digital Collection, Park City Museum.

daily but didn't realize that every community in America had one or more service stations that this comic strip could have been based upon.

I didn't know Johnny Fritch and he didn't know me. Still, he hired me on the spot. He gave me a short lesson on how to pump gas, check oil, ring up sales on the cash register, and said I'd work out. Then he said he be back around closing time, hopped into his car and drove off, leaving me in charge.

Thank God business was slow. I really had no idea what to do, so I swept the floor and, before the day was done, had washed the windows.

Around 5 p.m. or so, McFarland and Hullinger's dump trucks began showing up. McFarland and Hullinger, an ore-hauling firm located in Tooele, Utah, employed a crew of Park City natives to haul old low-grade mine tailings that were used in the smelting process as a form of flux.

Fritch had forgotten to tell me about them. There were five or six trucks and they lined up behind one another waiting to be filled with gas. I kept the gas pump running and put them all on one receipt. I soon discovered that washing windshields on big trucks is a lot harder than on cars. At night they were parked behind the garage, except the ones than needed work done on them.

About this time of day, Cliff Ashcraft would show up. He was the mechanic who maintained this fleet of trucks. He was in his mid-50s, maybe younger, with weathered features, and seldom smiled. He was always dressed in gray-striped coveralls.

Cliff was married to Mary Horrocks Ashcraft. Mary was a good Mormon and a great cook. Years later I would come to appreciate her kitchen talents when, as a member of the Park City Kiwanis Club, I ate many great meals she prepared at the War Memorial Building on Main Street.

Horan's was a one-bay service station; the work area was just large enough to handle one dump truck at a time. This work area shared a common wall with the rest of the station but had no interconnecting doorways. Come six o'clock I would turn off the gas pumps and the lights and lock the door, leaving Cliff alone in his half of the building to fine-tune his trucks.

It soon became a routine. During the summer on weekdays I'd work from noon until 6 p.m. Weekends were from 9 a.m. to 6 p.m. After school started in September, I would work from 4 to 6 p.m. and all day Saturday and Sunday. It was a great job; I got paid for handling what little business there was, and the rest of the time I could read.

The best part was that I had an excuse not to go out for football. I went out for football during my freshman and sophomore years in high school and hated it. It was one of those peer-pressure things; nearly every boy in my class went out.

It was a given that the good, semi-new gear went to the players who actually had a chance to play. The rest of us were issued uniforms that were awfully old, way too big, and stank like all hell.

My shoes were so big that the toes curved up and the front cleat looked like the horn of a prehistoric beast.

We followed the same routine every day: two laps around the field, then twenty minutes or so of calisthenics, or until you worked up a good sweat. Then, just as the sun disappeared behind Iron Mountain, you got to sit on the cold ground and shiver while watching the A team scrimmage. My job was a great excuse to escape this suffering and put a little money in my pocket.

My first great concern with this job was not knowing when payday was. After about ten days or so, I got up my courage and asked Johnny when and how I got paid. I guess the troubled look on my face gave him a good laugh. He told me that was my responsibility. I should keep track of my hours, then take my pay from the cash register and leave a note showing my hours worked and pay taken at 50 cents per hour. It worked great for me.

It was as though I was my own boss. I loved to read and at times I had hours on end to satisfy my obsession. I probably neglected my job some because of this.

Once a stranger stopped by, bought a little gas and asked me to check under the hood. I checked his oil, which was okay. I told him so and soon was back engrossed in the book I was reading. The stranger in turn drove up the street and doubled back, stopping at Mawhinney Motor, where he asked the attendant, Dean Hansen, to check under the hood.

Dean was a classmate and one smart kid. He spied a worn-out fan belt and brought it to the driver's attention.

The driver was the Gates Mystery Man! At that time the Gates Rubber Company had a promotion in which an employee would drive around the country in a car with an obviously worn fan belt or bad coolant hose. If the service-station attendant spotted the problem and pointed it out to the driver, the attendant would be rewarded with a prize of up to five silver dollars.

I can't remember how much Dean received. But I do know he never let me forget how I missed the Mystery Man but he didn't. The hell of it is, I forget the name of the book that I was reading. It seemed so important at the time.

The only real excitement I had at Horan's Station came one day in the autumn when I was getting ready to close up. A cowboy rode up, hopped off his horse and hitched her to the gas pump. I was getting ready to tease him by asking, "Do you want me to fill her up?"

Then I really looked at him. Though he hadn't shaved for several days, I could see he was as white as a sheet. He asked, "You got a phone?" I nodded yes and pointed to the pay phone hanging from the wall.

He shook his head no, adding, "I ain't got no money – and I need to call the sheriff." He wasn't yelling or anything, but I could feel his stress.

Now this caught my full attention, and all thought of locking up vanished.

"The sheriff is in Coalville, but I could call the city police. What do you want them for, anyway?"

"I found a dead woman back yonder on the hill."

He was motioning towards the east. I grabbed the phone and waited for the operator to come on the line. Seconds seem like minutes when you're in a hurry. Soon that professional voice chimed in, "Number please."

"Operator, I need the police. Can you send him down to Horan's old station?"

"What is the nature of the emergency?" she asked, still keeping the professional tone.

"There a cowboy here who found a dead woman up on the Masonic Mountain."

The cowboy was shaking his head at me. I knew he had additional information, so I handed him the phone.

"I ain't no cowboy – I herd sheep!" he told her and handed the phone back to me, muttering, "I don't want anyone getting the wrong idea about me."

I had heard that cattlemen and sheep people didn't get along with one another; now I knew it was true.

Taking the phone, I announced, "I'm back."

She replied, "I found him, Gary. I'll send him right down."

I was wondering how she knew who I was. But it's true that the phone operators in Park City knew more about what was going on in Park City than the rest of the town combined.

I told the sheepherder that the police were on the way. A short time later two cars pulled up and parked outside; neither was the police car. News travels fast in small towns. A minute or two later the cop car skidded to a halt and Bob Evans, the city marshal, turned off his siren and pushed his way into the station, only to be brushed aside by the sheepherder, who was headed outside to calm his frightened horse. "Damn fool!" he muttered loud enough for all to hear while looking at Evans.

He soon explained that his dog had discovered the remains of a dead woman a couple of hundred yards above the city's trash dump. By now there were five or six cars and a dozen or so people gathered around. They all left at once. It was a regular stampede to the trash dump.

Of course, I was going too, just as fast as I could finish locking up. But Cliff, the mechanic, had crawled out from under one of the dump trucks and wanted to know what was going on. It took me a good five minutes to satisfy his curiosity.

I think I ran all the way to the trash dump, and started the steep climb up to where the crowd was gathered. While I was on my way up, some were already coming down. Someone remarked to me in passing, "You don't want to see that – come back with us."

That got me moving a little faster. I thought, they think I'm some sort of sissy and want to protect me. I'll show them.

You know, sometimes I should listen to people. Most of the dead woman's face was eaten away by God knows what, and she was bloated and seemed ready to explode. And the odor – oh God, did it stink!

Ray Wortley, whose Wortley Brothers trucking company was a competitor of McFarland and Hullinger, was there in typical form, loud and cynical. Looking around at his Cozy Tavern cronies, he said, "Well, I'll take her first. Who's got second?"

I made my retreat without calling attention to myself. I made a mental note to keep away from Ray Wortley.

Wortley held court at the Cozy several times each week, but more often than not he could be found spreading his form of humor at Lower Pop Jenks. At Lower Pop's his language was not quite as salty as he used in the Cozy, but it was raunchy enough to turn many heads.

Rippon, the local mortician, placed the corpse in a plastic bag and put it into a freezer, hoping she would be identified at a later date. To my knowledge that never happened. I believe she was disposed of when the Olpin Mortuary bought his establishment.

Fritch soon closed Horan's Station and I started work at his rebuilt garage shortly thereafter.

Fritch's Garage was north on Park Avenue, a couple of hundred yards outside the city limits. It was on the west side of the road where it connected with U.S. Highway 40 (now Kearns Boulevard). It was among a cluster of three service stations and two restaurants – or what we called road houses.

Located next to Fritch's was Coffee John's café. Across the highway and to the east of Fritch's was Eley Motorway Service. Located to the north of Eley's was Tommy St. Jeor's Conoco Service, and between the two other service stations was Lower Pop Jenks Café.

The finishing touches to Fritch's building were still going on and I got to help. In doing so I got acquainted with a mixed bag of personalities.

One day I worked with Swede (Albert) Carlson, a white-haired widower who must have been pushing 80 years of age. I loved his accent when he called me "Getty." He had the bluest eyes I think I have ever seen.

That old man worked the hell out of me; I had a hard time just trying to keep up with him. We were digging out the pit that housed the coal-burning furnace. It was still filled with ash, dirt and refuse from the fire.

I came to hate that furnace. It was my job to fill the stoker (its brand name was Stoker-Matic) with slack coal. The part I hated was cleaning the furnace of "clinkers" made up of ash that had fused together in lumps. When the furnace door was opened, the pit would fill with smoke and the smoke was laced with the odor of sulfur. Fritch bought coal that was mined nearby in Coalville, Utah. It was notorious for its high-sulfur content.

By the time I had finished, I smelled like a burnt match. It really bothered me on Fridays when there was a school dance that followed a basketball game. I shouldn't have worried. I soon discovered my cigarette smoke covered the sulfur smell. At least one girl told me so.

I also got to work with Slim Wheeler, who stood about 6-foot-5 and was skinny as a rail. Slim was hired as a handyman by Jenks Nelson and lived at his ranch, which was located where the base of Park City Mountain Resort now stands.

As a ranch hand Slim was a failure. Jenks fired him but let him live at the ranch. I was surprised to discover that he was hard working and a good carpenter. He did all the finish work in Fritch's showroom.

One of the others who helped put the building back into shape was Bud Gasparac, a part-time stonemason. Bud built a beautiful flagstone counter in the showroom. For a while it sure did look good. But in the long run it proved to be not so satisfying. Flagstone, when given a chance, will suck up oil or any petroleum-based product.

Bud worked a variety of jobs during his life, including heavy-equipment operator, stonemason and aircraft pilot. He made many attempts to get the city to support the building of an airport out by what is now known as Quinn's Junction. He finally took charge of the Utoco tank farm, located on lower Park Avenue just north of Iron Horse Drive.

This was a lucrative business during the late 1940s and early '50s. By then, many of the homes and businesses had switched from coal to heating oil to heat their homes. Gasparac, being in town, had an advantage over other "bulk" deliverers.

Dad eventually put an oil stove in our living room. It took the place of our old coal-burning parlor stove, but only in function. It lacked both beauty and elegance. There were no more crackling sounds, and the view of the flames was soon obscured by soot on its window. It was not until after the advent of the ski resort that natural gas came to Park City in 1964.

Fritch also owned the Utah Mine, a silver-and-lead mine out by Callao in the far western part of Utah. He was trying to develop it on a shoestring budget. A few times each year he would recruit a crew of some of Park City's derelicts and take them out to his desert mine and let them work at their own pace.

I believe they loved it out there. There were hot springs in the region, where the men could bathe or just lie around, and Fritch supplied them with good food and an occasional jug or two of cheap booze. I never heard any of them complaining.

I use the term "derelicts" loosely, but it was quite true. When people were fleeing Park City for greener pastures, there was a whole group of men who for many reasons were stuck in the camp. They lacked families, money and youth. Many had health issues, some were drunkards, and nearly all believed that good times were right around the corner. In reality there was no governmental support.

John E. Fritch was a grand man. He was born in Croatia and said he was a "bohunk." When I told him a few of my friends were bohunks, he corrected me, saying that to be a bohunk you had to be born in the "Old Country." That made sense to me, but I never corrected my friends who were proud of their heritage.

His family name was Frkovich, but when he went into business he Americanized it. First he named himself John E. Smith, but came to believe his name should reflect his Croatian roots but still sound American. He settled on Fritch, but kept the "John E." part. "E." stood for nothing, but it looked good on paper, and that way people could call him John E. or Johnny; either way it sounded good.

Johnny told me that when his parents moved to Utah, his father operated a small neighborhood grocery in Murray. But times were tough and he was forced to close the store and move to Park City, where he found work at the Daly Mine. He died later from "miners' con" (silicosis). As Johnny explained it, management took full advantage of the "dumb foreigners," especially those from Eastern Europe, and gave them the dirtiest jobs in the mine. He indicated that the bohunk community pulled together and helped out one another until times improved.

Jackie Rukavina, Fritch's mechanic and body-and-fender man, was also of Croatian heritage; they were neighbors and lived high up on Daly Avenue in Empire Canyon.

I remember both Johnny's and Jackie's mothers. They brought their customs and dress from Croatia and seemed to live in their own private world. Often they could be seen early in the morning on the west side of Daly Avenue, sitting on a bench chopped out of a log that had been placed there many years earlier for miners who walked to their jobs.

The two old ladies, shawls covering their heads, with long dresses and black shoes that reached over their ankles, would sit warming themselves in the early sunlight and smoking small white clay pipes. I probably remember this because it was the only time I have ever seen women smoking pipes.

Jackie was a good mechanic, an excellent body-and-fender man, and a competent painter. He took charge of all the wrecked cars that Fritch took in, beating out the dents, welding, grinding, sanding, and then painting the finished products to look as though they had just come off the assembly line.

Jackie was clean living, with no bad habits. I once asked him if he had ever had been drunk. He said yes. He told me that during Prohibition, when he was about my age, he and his buddies would search under the seats of cars for booze. They usually poured out the bootleg stuff and sold the bottles back to the bootleggers. But one time he decided to try what they were dumping out and drank his fill.

Jackie said he became violently ill and passed out. He told me he was unconscious for five days and bedridden for many weeks, and that many people thought it was a miracle that he lived. I had heard that many people died of this type of poisoning during the era, but Jackie was the only person I ever met who had an experience with it.

Jackie's only passion that I know of was fly-fishing. Often, when he got off work at 5 p.m., he would drive out to Strawberry Reservoir in the Uinta Basin – a four-hour round trip – for an hour of fishing. In some respects, I'm envious of anyone with that much devotion to a sport or hobby.

Fritch had the automobile dealership for Dodge and Plymouth cars. I got the honor of washing and polishing each new car as it came in, making it ready for the showroom. But my main job was still taking care of the out-front business: gas, oil, occasional grease and oil changes, plus fixing a few flat tires.

The comic strip Gasoline Alley could have gotten its inspiration from Fritch's Garage. It was a gathering place for car junkies. It really was a diverse group that gathered there. The young, the old, the well-off and the dire poor all had questions and needed advice about their cars. Others would show up just for conversation, a place to hang out. I got to know many, and learn much.

Fritch once bought a couple of Navy war-surplus submersible pumps to use in his mine. He then discovered they were wired for DC current. So he recruited three Park City natives who worked rebuilding electric motors at General Electric's repair shop in Salt Lake – his son, Clyde Fritch, along with Wayne Goff and Gene Florence – to rewrap these motors so they could run on AC electric current. It took months working weekends to rebuild these pumps, and I was fascinated watching their progress. It was a finicky operation laying these fine-gauge copper wires in place. I believe it would have been easier learning the art of weaving a Persian rug than wrapping an electric motor.

The garage gang (whoever was present) would take a coffee break at 10 a.m., then again at 2 p.m., and walk across the street to Pop Jenks Café. I was never included in these breaks. That was one of the reasons I had a job there – to tend to business while they were away. Still, I wished I could have sat in on those bull sessions.

I remember once hearing "Slat" Thompson explain, as they were heading over to Pop Jenks, the need to have a chain attached to the tank on his oil-tank truck to drain off static electricity. He claimed that one night he had left off the chain and could see huge electric sparks jumping from his tanker truck and lighting up the sky. The whole group was hooting with laughter and asking him to prove his story. Damn, I'd like to know how that one was resolved.

One person who bought gas at the station was Tom Costas. Tom was the mayor of Park City during the mid-1950s. Being a politician, he spread his gas purchases among all the stations in town. For years he was president of the local mining union, United Steelworkers of America Local No. 4264, and then became involved in the management of the New Park Mine Company. During my time with Fritch, Costas was developing mining property – mostly uranium – on his own. This was during the uranium boom of the 1950s.

Most citizens loved him; others hated him. It depended on what side your toast was buttered on. While head of the union, he talked members out of going on strike for several months (the union contract had expired and the miners were working without one) while the mines stockpiled enough ore to keep them in business. There was an old saying, "Costas cost us our jobs!" He went on to do assessment work and acquire new claims for the New Park Mine Company.

One afternoon Costas pulled in next to the gas pumps and I ran out to service his car. He was driving a big, white, brand-new two-door Packard Caribbean sedan. Fritch followed me out from his office to admire the car. He asked Costas how much money it cost. Costas told him he swapped 10,000 shares of stock in his tungsten mine in central Utah for the car.

Fritch started laughing, and laughed so hard that tears streamed down his face. He had a hard time staying on his feet. As far as Fritch knew and as I was learning, no tungsten has ever been mined in Utah. Yes, Costas was good at what he did.

Fritch did get quite a few customers who were traveling on U.S. 40. Most just wanted gas to get back on the road; very few showed any interest about where they had stopped.

I remember a middle-aged couple pulling in late one afternoon right after a heavy rain shower. The sun came out from behind the clouds. The city's trash dump, which was located on the hillside a mile to the southeast, was usually dull and covered with smoke from perpetual fires. But after this shower the glistening sunlight was reflected by thousands of tin cans. It was a wondrous display.

The woman started taking photos of the scene. I told the husband that his wife was taking pictures of the trash pile. She overheard me and said, "I don't care. It's ... it's beautiful!" It's possible that she was Park City's first non-mining and pre-skiing tourist.

Often people would stop in, asking for directions. The number-one request often came from cowboy-type young men: "How do I get to the whorehouses from here?" And I would give them directions to madam Bessie Wheeler's house. Once, though, when I was locking up and I was sure I would not be there if he returned, I gave a man directions to the house of Eugene McCusker, the high school principal. I've wondered for a lifetime if the cowboy knocked on his door, and if so, what happened.

I worked for Fritch through high school and on weekends during my freshman year in college. And I really believe I learned more there than I did in school. It was a good experience.

The Battle of Big Four

The author dressed for combat in his snappy cowboy outfit.
Photo courtesy of the Kimball Archive.

I was a member of the so-called gun culture way before they had a name for it. Fortunately, if you live long enough, you might outgrow your past and the nickname name that came with it. However, I really did love that nickname.

Way back when, almost before I can remember, I was given a nickname that I carried well into my twenties. Even now a few good friends use "Gunzee" as a term of friendship. Few knew where it came from; most thought it was from my ability with – and love of – guns. I didn't discourage them, and in some respects they were not completely wrong. I did have a great love of guns. It's possible I inherited this from my dad.

Anyway, back on my fourth or fifth birthday, I was given a snappy cowboy outfit that consisted of two cap guns with a belt and holsters to match. When anyone would ask who I was, I'd tell them, "I'm Two-Gun Kimball."

Unfortunately, I had a hell of a speech impediment. Back in those days everyone called it being "tongue-tied." My pronunciation of Two-Gun Kimball came out sounding something like "GunzeeKingo" – at least, that's how Ralph Erickson, a neighbor, pronounced it. He started calling me GunzeeKingo and it caught on. At least the Gunzee part did.

In my teenage years it seemed that all my friends had .22 caliber rifles, and depending on the time of year there was always something different to shoot at. There were Rocky Mountain ground squirrels that everyone called "potguts" that were once common in this area in spring and summer. Rabbits were not only abundant in autumn and winter, they were also good eating. And the rats at the city garbage dump were plentiful all year long. Not only that, but when we turned 16 and could drive, it was a great way to pick up girls. The simple invitation, "You want to go to the trash pile and shoot rats?" was never turned down. Either Park City girls were "boy crazy" or the love of shooting ran deep in their veins.

Most of the time that I went out shooting, it was with neighborhood kids; most were a year or two younger than me. Unlike them, who only had single-shot .22 rifles, I usually had my brother's pump .22. Oh, it was a wonderful gun. You could hold the trigger down and the gun would fire as fast as you could pump it.

Of course, I seldom hit what I was aiming at, but, boy, could you make the dust dance and the sagebrush sway to the music of bang, bang, bang. I'd explain that, even though I missed the can or bottle I fired at, if it had been a charging bear or cougar, I would have hit it more than once. My younger friends were always impressed.

One chilly autumn day, several of my classmates came by, said they were going rabbit hunting down at the Big Four, and asked if I wanted to go with them. The area we called the Big Four was on the flats below Park City, just south of where the Summit County Justice Center now stands. It was filled with mill tailings, scrub oak and bunch grass. The only access was by a railroad frontage road and a few rutted sheep trails.

At that time there was no Silver Creek Junction. Back then U.S. Highway 40 skirted Park City on the road we now call Kearns Boulevard. The Big Four area always seemed cold, windswept and desolate. On this day even the rabbits seemed to have deserted it.

I had never hunted with these boys before and was delighted that they had asked me. We pretty much followed the railroad tracks all the way down, taking a few shots here and there at magpies.

Magpies were a much-maligned scavenger that the county would pay a bounty of 10 cents a head for. I never heard of anyone collecting the bounty. Money-wise it did not make sense. It cost nearly a dollar for a box of .22 shells, and it usually took nearly a box to hit one. You might part a few feathers, but to actually hit one was a real feat. Then you would have to collect nearly a hundred heads to pay for a trip to Coalville, and by the time you gathered that many they probably would really stink.

Anyway, I was quite relieved to discover that they were no better marksmen than me. We scared up a few sage hens, but missed them by a mile. We spotted what we thought was a rabbit, and I tried to impress them with my rapid pump shots. I did hit something – probably a sandbag left by a railroad work crew. My classmates laughed, but it actually seemed they were laughing with me.

Somehow or other we kinda divided up into teams and had a mock gun battle. Not shooting to hit one another, but seeing how close you could come without doing any damage. I was with Roy Hamilton; we were hiding in some sort of a pit. Our opponents – Arvil Price, Frank Provost and Jim Kinsey – were somewhere behind a semi-fallen wooden fence.

Well, it seemed that Hamilton was a lousy shot. He announced in a whisper, "If that's one, I got him," and squeezed off a shot. Just like in the movies, Kinsey let out a scream and, I swear, flew five feet backwards!

It became a scary scene. Everyone was yelling, "No more shooting!" "Hold your fire!" "You crazy bastards – you shot Kinsey!"

Kinsey begged for someone to hand him his gun so he could get even. Finally, he settled down to accept the reality that we were all in for a bad time.

We agreed on a story as to how he got shot, and that was while climbing over a fence. Or I should say that Kinsey had already climbed over the fence and Hamilton, following close behind, slipped and his gun went off and shot Kinsey in the rump. I guess I didn't mention that before: it was a perfect rear-end shot.

(Years later Hamilton joined the Marine Corps. They soon recognized his gift and made him a "BAR-Man." That is what they called the grunts who carried Browning Automatic Rifles. At the time, it was said, their life expectancy in combat was five minutes.)

We all knew that, if the truth were found out, we would be in for it – from our parents, from our peers, from the police; God knows how far it would go. And even worse than the punishment would be becoming the laughing stock of a whole community.

Someone said, "We've got to cover one another's backsides."

Kinsey piped up, "Okay, but keep Hamilton off mine."

Everyone laughed, and we started to make our way back to town. It was a hard walk for Kinsey, but we finally got to U.S. 40, and it was not long before we hitched a ride. I don't remember who the driver was, but it was a pickup truck, and after we explained what had happened he dumped us off at the Miners Hospital.

Dr. Dan Oniki was the town doctor at that time. He came to Park City in 1949 and in a short time won the community over. He was a soft-spoken Japanese-American with a reputation for being very competent. We just hoped he would buy our story and wouldn't turn us over to the authorities. And I guess it was in the back of our minds as to who would pay and how much it would cost.

Shown here, starting from top left, are the author and his comrades in arms at the Battle of Big Four: Roy Hamilton, Gary Kimball, Jim Kinsey, Arvil Price, and Frank Provost. These photos are taken from the 1952 Park City High School yearbook. Notice that Hamilton, Kimball and Kinsey are all wearing the same tie. Photographer Kendall Webb would bring a spare tie to lend to boys who had failed to dress for the occasion.

He ushered Kinsey into an examining room and didn't seem to mind that we tagged along. His nurse was already there getting things ready. She was a very attractive young lady who was only a few years older than us. She looked efficient in her crisp white uniform, her nursing cap perched nearly on the back of her head. Horn-rim glasses and a pencil tucked neatly in her hair above her ear gave her an image of authority.

Dr. Oniki instructed Kinsey to undress from the waist down. The nurse swabbed the wound with a disinfectant.

Dr. Oniki located the bullet. It had nearly passed through a cheek and was within a quarter-inch of the surface. Fortunately, no bones were hit. He cut an X-shaped incision and, with some long tweezers – I think they're called forceps – he removed the bullet. He then filled a large syringe with saline solution and flushed the wound clean. With a stitch or two on both ends, the patch job was complete.

In the following days, I kept quiet and waited, hoping my parents would not hear about this episode. Oh how I prayed the story would not be reported in *The Park Record*. They often reported on who was in the hospital and why, but this story evaded them. I don't know if the gunshot was reported to the state. For some reason, we seldom talked about it among ourselves.

I guess I have always been a slow learner, and my junior year in high school easily proves the point. We got a new shop teacher, Raymond Childs, who was hired straight from the Utah State Reform School. I guess the Park City School Board believed his predecessor, Waldo Peterson, wasn't quite up to the job. He seemed to have problems with many of his students.

We took to calling Mr. Childs "The Chief." The movie "Blackboard Jungle" had recently been released and there was a scene where Glenn Ford, playing the teacher, was referred to as the chief. I don't know if Mr. Childs knew of that, or if he cared.

He evidently had some connections from his time teaching at the reform school that gave him access to some war-surplus "lab coats." They were great. For just a dollar we could buy a knee-length denim coat that had large lettering on both the front and back reading "POW" (Prisoner of War).

Those who had cars could work on them in the school shop, and Mr. Childs offered rudimentary instructions in using the arc welder.

I had just finished reading a novel about a street gang known as the Amboy Dukes and how they had made a weapon they called a zip gun. I think it shot bicycle spokes or some such silly thing. I knew I could do better than that.

I took some ¾-inch wood dowel and cut off a chunk about six inches long. I found a drill bit that was about the size of a .22 caliber bullet and drilled a barrel. I wrapped the full length of the barrel with two layers of black electrical tape. Then, to be on the safe side, I wrapped the whole thing with blasting wire. Anywhere else, people would have used bailing wire, but in mining camps there was always a lot of blasting wire available. It seemed every home had a spool or two lying around.

For the gun frame I used one of my old cap guns. The hardest part of my project was spot-welding a tack on the hammer of the gun to act as the firing pin. I probably burned through the better part of two welding rods before I got the tack securely in place. Securing the barrel took some time, but when I finished I really had a frightening instrument.

Several of my classmates wanted to watch the first firing of my gun. The problem was I didn't have any .22 cartridges. Frank Provost said he had a box and his yard would be a perfect place for the demonstration. His home was the highest house on Sampson Avenue. Frank's father, Roland, always claimed it was high enough on Treasure Hill to be just out of the city limits.

It's funny how far you can stretch your arm away from your body when the gun you're going to fire might blow up. Provost, Hamilton and Price were a good ten feet behind me. With my eyes shut, and shielding my face with my free hand, I fired.

BOOM!

I didn't see where the bullet hit, but my friends assured me I hit the mountainside – a pretty hard thing to miss when the whole yard was facing the mountain. The achievement of building a gun from scratch that actually worked brought on back-patting that really made a person feel good. And now they all were clamoring for a turn at firing the gun. Since it was Frank's yard and his bullets, he got the first turn.

This time no one was hiding; we crowded around Frank as he took careful aim at a tin can and gently pulled the trigger.

BROOM!

The barrel blew apart into a thousand splinters, blasting wire littered the yard, and the cap-gun hammer disappeared, never to be found. Frank just stood there, eyes and mouth wide open. There was a kinda blank stare on his face.

I think the only thing that saved me from a beating was Frank's mother, Tina. She came charging out the door, screaming and demanding to know what was going on, then lit into a tirade about the danger of firecrackers and blasting caps. It turned into a full-blown lecture. The last words I heard as I ran down the hill towards home were, "No more explosions!"

I bet I was home before she finished her lecture. My gunsmithing days were over before they really began. And like everything in my life, I was poorer but a little bit wiser.

As far as guns go, I slowly gave them up. It was a slow evolution, and now I'm puzzled why it took so long.

Once, shortly after President Kennedy was assassinated, I even circulated a petition championing gun rights for the NRA. My father, a loyal member and supporter of the NRA, brought me the petition to collect signatures. At the time I was operating a small corner grocery store, was the agent for a popular insurance company, and was in contact with many people.

I collected more than two hundred signatures. I only encountered one person who refused to sign it, and I think he declined because I had refused to give him a case of beer on credit a few days earlier. But he could have had moral principles I was unaware of.

When I totally quit guns, it came quite suddenly. It happened during a deer hunt. It was cold, I was tired, and it suddenly dawned on me while watching my partner clean his newly killed buck. As I watched the steam pour off the guts, and the blood and the overpowering odor seeping from an animal that only a few minutes earlier had been grand to look upon, it struck me that what I was doing was wrong. It was not fun, and to call it a sport was beyond logic. And the same applies to other types of hunting.

I'm still a meat eater, and if that makes me a hypocrite, so be it. I'm still evolving, and maybe someday my taste buds will catch up with my newfound morals. Guns have only one purpose, and that is to kill! The news is filled with the carnage caused by gun violence; every day we are saturated with it.

I can actually remember when the NRA magazine, *The American Rifleman*, was filled with articles about hunting and tips on gun safety. I now wonder when and how it turned into a hate-mongering organization more reminiscent of Nazi brown shirts than the red hunting garb of the past generation. They make my stupid gun-blunder stories – that could have caused death – an amusing joke. I firmly believe that 99 percent of NRA membership lack the mental or moral capacity of the 16-year-old kids I wrote about in this tale.

Santos Giauguitio

Only a few of the shacks on Easy Street had running water.
Electricity usually consisted of a single bulb dangling from the ceiling,
and the toilet was often an outhouse built over Poison Creek.
Photo courtesy of the Patricia E. Smith Collection, Park City Museum.

Santos Giauguitio is a name that does not easily roll off the lips. Few people knew his last name. *The Park Record*, for its readers' sake, or perhaps through its own ignorance, referred to him as John Santos. Only once could I find a reference in the archives to Santos Giauguitio.

When I knew Santos, he was in his late fifties, maybe older. By any standard he was a strange fellow: small in stature, about five-foot-four, and always in need of a bath and clean clothing. He was usually two or three days late shaving, as his salt-and-pepper growth testified. In cold weather he wore a heavy coat that draped far below his knees, accompanied by a hunter's-style cap with the earmuffs pulled over his ears. His dark eyes were highlighted by whites that seemed to grow larger with his stare as he talked to you.

Santos was one of the three or four people I knew who lived on Easy Street, a rutted, unplatted road below Heber Avenue on the bank of Poison Creek.

I really did not know Santos until we opened the Grubstake Grocery store on the southwest corner of Heber and Park avenues. My partner, Bill Henrion, and I rented the old storefront from Bart and Stella Duke. Their home was in the back part of the building.

The store was not large – a room about 20 by 16 feet. The front windows were heavy-gauge plate glass. It actually looked more like a store from the outside. On the inside, there was much to be desired.

It was heated by a miniature cast-iron potbelly stove. During the winter it would burn about one large gunnysack of slack coal per week. The staircase leading to the locked door of the Dukes' residence took up about five percent of the store's floor space. There was no plumbing, meaning no restroom, which could make a shift awful long. Other than that, our store was a typical corner grocery store.

We were an evening-and-weekend operation. When the other grocery stores on Main Street closed at 6 p.m., we prospered, more or less. At least, that was our business plan. I wonder if business plans ever work.

The bread-and-milk trade was great. Trouble is, you could starve on it. So we put in a complete line of penny candy, and toys of all sorts. To this day, when I meet people who were children then, they still refer to the Grubstake market as "the candy store."

We obtained a beer license, becoming the first market in Park City to do so. (Up until then, beer was sold only from saloons.) We started a second-hand bookstore, buying used paperback books for 10 cents and selling them for 25 cents. Westerns, mysteries and romance novels were popular; most of the other books ended up at home with me. We even obtained a license to sell firearms after a customer who owed us money used his hunting rifle to pay off his debt. We obtained a few other rifles from customers and for a while it looked as though we were becoming a pawnshop.

On holidays such as July 4th and Labor Day, helium balloons and firecrackers were a must. On the eve of one Independence Day, Bill brought in a dozen starter revolvers. They looked like real guns but shot only blanks. For our clientele the five-dollar price tag was steep, and most sat in a display case gathering dust.

I remember the first time Santos came in. He wanted to know how long we had been there. I told him about a year. He then asked why he didn't know about it. I shrugged and told him we had an ad in *The Park Record*. But that wasn't good enough for him. He got really mad and left in a huff, muttering that I should have told him.

After that rough start, Santos became a customer of sorts. About every other week he would come in and would always want a pint of strawberry ice cream. We carried Hi-Land Dairy products, and for the most part the company was great in supplying our needs. But most customers bought ice cream by the quart at least. Hi-Land did supply us with pints of vanilla and chocolate ice cream, and on occasion had strawberry in pints, but not often. It was a slow mover.

Don't tell that to Santos. He loved strawberry ice cream, but the quart was too large. It would melt before he could finish it.

I doubt there was one shack on Easy Street that had a refrigerator. Only a few of them had running water. Electricity usually consisted of a single bulb dangling from the ceiling, and the toilet was often an outhouse built over Poison Creek.

I understood his plight and frustration, but was at a loss as to how to help him. Except to stand there and be yelled at.

One particular day Santos came in. I don't recall his purchase, but he paid for it and left. A few minutes later he was back, claiming he had given me a twenty-dollar bill and didn't get the right change. He claimed I had cheated him!

Well, I checked the till to see if there were any twenty-dollar bills in it. (There seldom were. That was back in the day when a twenty-dollar bill got respect.) After a few minutes of intense argument, Santos left in a huff. It's not fun being accused of being a crook, but I chalked it up to being all in a day's work.

A week or so later, Santos was back, made a purchase and then came back again, claiming that he had paid with a twenty, and that I had cheated him once more! Again he left in a huff.

I was at my wits' end. It really bothered me, and from that time on, if we had no customers and I saw Santos walking towards the store, I would lock the door and turn off the lights. Santos would rattle the door, peek through the window, then knock. In time he would leave and I would reopen. Probably not the best business practice, but it worked for me.

One day, while I was in the post office, Santos was just leaving the window. I asked Jerry Hanley, the postal clerk, if he had had any strange dealings with Santos.

Jerry started to chuckle. "You mean the twenty-dollar bill?"

"Ya," I replied.

Jerry said it was about a once-a-month occurrence, and nearly every business in town had a similar experience. Knowing others were plagued with the same problem made me feel better. From then on I wouldn't lock the door if I saw him coming. From then on I would be pleasant but stern.

Strangely, Santos never did the twenty-dollar-bill thing again, and stopped screaming about us not having strawberry ice cream in pints. He would buy a variety of Popsicles and seemed happy with his purchases. Then one day he came in and wanted to buy a gun. I asked him why he wanted a gun.

His reply: "I'm going to shoot the son-o-bitch Lake guy. He's stealin' my things."

I knew Arnold Lake. He lived on Easy Street and he was a decent sort of guy. I had heard he was an epileptic and had other health problems. The only thing I knew about him for sure was that he was a reader. He went through the stack of Western paperback books we had, was all but through the mystery books, and joked that if we didn't get some new books he would have to start on the romance novels.

I asked Santos how he knew Lake was stealing. He reached deep into his pocket and produced a gold ring that had a piece of string tied to it. He said, "I dangle my magic ring into a glass of water, hold real still, and ask it the question, 'Is son-o-bitch Lake stealin' my things?' The ring starts to turn clock way. That means yes. The other way means no."

He continued, "I want to buy that gun," pointing to one of the dust-covered starting pistols. I reached into the display case and retrieved the gun.

"I can sell it to you but it won't do you much good. It's a starting revolver."

Santos stared at me intently. "What you mean?"

I tried to explain what a starter gun was. I got out a small round box the size of a snuff tobacco container that held the starter shells. They were .22-caliber size, a little shorter than a .22 short bullet, and pinched closed at the front. I handed Santos the gun to show that the barrel was not drilled through and told him the guns were for starting races.

Santos turned red and his eyes seemed to grow larger. "You son-o-bitch, you can't sell phony guns! I'm telling the police you sell phony guns! They start races with real guns, you son-o-bitch.

I'm not buyin' a phony gun. It's against the law!" He shoved the gun back at me and, again, left in a huff.

For the longest time I pondered if I should report this incident to the police. I decided I would mention it in casual conversation while having coffee at Lower Pop Jenks Café. The place was a haunt for most officers. Sheriff's deputies, highway patrol and the local city police, they all knew where to find good coffee.

I don't know if the law talked to him, or if no one would sell him a gun, or if he changed his mind about shooting Lake. But, thank God, he didn't do it. Lake was our best book customer.

About a year or so later – I don't remember the circumstance – Santos was admitted into the Veterans' Hospital in Salt Lake City. I was surprised that he was a veteran; no one ever mentioned the fact, and that's unusual in a small town like Park City.

At the time my wife Jane was a nurse at the hospital. She would often carpool with a male nurse, Paul Olsen. One Sunday afternoon, Paul dropped by our house for a visit. Jane and Paul were talking about the long commute, their dislike of shift work, and other aspects of their jobs.

Paul started laughing and looked at me. "Did you ever know a guy from Park City by the name Santos?"

I replied that I knew him well, and could hardly wait for Paul to tell me his Santos tale so I could tell him mine.

Paul, still chuckling, continued, "Well, one night last week a leggy blonde nurse was trying to get Santos to his bed. She said, 'Now Santos, it's time for us to go to bed.'

"Santos looked at her, shaking his head no, and said, 'Jesus Christ woman, I got no five dollars. What's wrong with you?'"

Five dollars for years was the standard price in Park City's whorehouses.

The Kamas Rose

In the 1950s this building, 402 Main Street, was a tavern known as The Drift. When Kendall Webb took this photo in the late 1940s it was the Snow Ball Café. At this writing it is the Java Cow Café & Bakery.
Photo courtesy of the Kendall Webb Collection, Park City Museum.

Back in the late 1950s and early '60s, the Rose became a fixture on Park City's Main Street. I never knew her real name; some in Park City called her the Kamas Rose. In Kamas, it was said, she was known as River Rose.

Slight of build, she wore her straight brown stringy hair cropped unevenly several inches below her ears. Makeup was an item she never bought and seldom used. On occasion she would mooch some from a female patron in the saloons, then apply the rouge and lipstick in a heavy, if misguided, hand. She always seemed fairly happy with the results.

Rose appeared to be in her late thirties, but she could have been younger. The years had not been kind to her, but even her most severe critic would have had to admit that at one time or another she must have been pretty.

Rose had three passions: booze, smoking and fighting. She seemed driven in all three areas. What money she had she used for booze, and she spent freely. When she was drunk, she was mean, and it took little provocation to set her off on the course to a fight.

Quick of feet, and carrying a wallop with her fists, she usually gave better than she received. I knew of several big men who were terrified of her, not wanting to lose their hard-earned reputations by a defeat at her hands. It's understandable. What man would want to get tromped by a hundred-and-twenty-pound drunk named Rose?

Rose was a chain smoker, but she seldom paid for a pack of her own. She didn't like to mooch smokes from other patrons; for some reason she seemed to find this demeaning. So she would proposition any male that was handy with, "Hey, Bud, I'll lay ya for a pack of smokes."

Of course she was bluffing. Still, it's a most difficult situation to be caught in. I'm not sure how others handled it. I always pleaded poverty and offered her what few cigarettes I had with no strings attached.

She would pocket my pack but would often go on to the next male patron with the same offer. She always seemed to have plenty of cigarettes.

Rose usually wore a plain-print calico dress that was so soiled it could have stood upright under it own weight. One night she took up residence in The Drift tavern. Most saloons would tolerate her presence for only a short while before inviting her to leave, but the Drift did not scrutinize their customers with an eye for social acceptability. The only time they seemed to show concern was when a customer left the premises with money still in his pocket.

On this particular evening it seemed that a young, disgruntled, returned Mormon missionary was having seconds thoughts about his forthcoming marriage and was determined to have one last (or maybe his first) fling. The entire country has now adopted the Mormon attitude toward tobacco, but in that era smoking was generally accepted. In hindsight, I'm sure that if this particular young man had smoked, he would have been better off.

Rose propositioned this lad for a pack of smokes. As a nonsmoker, the boy could not resist the temptation of lecturing her on the evils of tobacco. He did offer to buy her a drink, however.

Now Rose didn't particularly like fighting her drinking companions, but she could not let his lecture go unanswered. She called the boy everything but a man and proclaimed that he didn't wear his pants proper and that they would look better on her.

Well, the boy, somewhat drunk, told Rose that she was not at all ladylike and should not disgrace the female form by wearing such a striking dress.

This discussion lasted through several more rounds of drinks. Finally the two headed out the door, in heated argument, and disappeared into the gloom of Swede Alley. After about 20 minutes they reappeared.

Taking small steps so that she would not step out of her oversized cowboy boots, Rose was quite becoming in her new outfit.

She was followed by the boy wearing Rose's calico dress, which really did not fit his form, and carrying her shoes, which were way too small. After the laughter of the house subsided, he continued his pleas to Rose.

She thought he looked cute. Besides, she said, "A deal is a deal, and I won't back out now."

The boy was rapidly sobering up and, to prevent gagging, had ceased sniffing his new clothes. He slowly came to the conclusion that he wasn't going to get his old clothes back. Choking back tears, he retreated to his car to seek the protection of his own culture. But as he fled, he damned the heathens of Park City at the top of his lungs.

After studying her new wardrobe with admiration in the backbar mirror, Rose decided that she was running low on smokes. She shifted down the bar to the next male patron.

Park Tavern Revisited

Mike Safianides and a female bartender behind the bar at the Park Tavern, 322 Main Street, in 1946. Since the early 1960s the building has been the home of Red Banjo Pizza. The tavern's back bar and cash register are still there.
Photo courtesy of the Kendall Webb Collection, Park City Museum.

My book, "Of Moths and Miners and Other Tales of Old Park City," was a good introduction to different establishments – saloons, cafés, and houses of ill repute – and their proprietors. This is my memory of a few of the characters who, in part, supported these institutions, and the Park Tavern in particular. In the 1950s, when Park City seemed to be on its last legs, many people with the means fled the town. After much of the dust had settled, there was one segment that remained. For the most part, it was made up of the old, and those who had outlived their families, or who never had families in the first place. One thing they all had in common was that this was their home. Most never thought about leaving.

Mike

With that said, I'm starting off with a story about Mike Safianides (April 9, 1884 – June 3, 1970), the cantankerous old Greek who owned the Park Tavern (now the home of Red Banjo Pizza). In "Of Moths and Miners and Other Tales of Old Park City," I have a story about Mike, but much was cut from the original story, and it would be a shame to see it lost forever.

Mike's broken English was hard on the ears and, at times, harder on your pocketbook. You never knew for sure what you had ordered until he brought it.

Mike could cuss like no other. One of his favorite oaths was, "Jesus o' Christ, you son o' bitch." Funny, when it was spoken in his Greek accent, it seemed more lyrical than insulting.

The rest of his oaths were so foreign to the ears that I could not make out one word. But there was no mistake. You knew it was cussing! Once, when I was showing several college exchange-student friends from Iran around Park City, we stopped in Mike's for a beer. It was not long before one of my friends asked in a whisper about Mike's nationality. I replied that he was Greek. My friend said, "He's cussing in Arabic with a lot of Turk thrown in, and I think there might be some Armenian, too."

When Mike was behind the bar, he was all business. There was no credit or "jawbone whiskey" – so named for the ability of a patron to talk himself into a free drink. He would stand for none of that. He was seldom on the other side of the bar – as a customer, that is – but when he was, he was jovial, and a big spender. It was a wonder to behold.

Mike had his soft spots. He was sentimental, and very patriotic. He was a proud Greek-American who boasted of becoming a citizen in 1928.

Once, when Bob Mawhinney, a good friend of mine, was home on leave from the Navy, he stopped in the Park Tavern to visit with Mike. Bob was a hospital man (medic) attached to the Marine Corps and was in a Marine uniform that night. Mike admired the uniform and pointed to his Marine "Semper Fidelis" tie clasp. Bob, without hesitation, handed the tie clasp to Mike.

Mike treasured that tie clasp. He wore it with every tie he owned and, when he wore no tie, the clasp was clipped to his shirt. I'm not positive, but I would bet it was buried with him.

Mike was born in Constantinople and grew to manhood under Ottoman Turk rule. He migrated to America shortly before the outbreak of World War I, around 1912. In 1958, on the eve of his retirement, he traveled to his home to visit family and friends. On disembarking from the aircraft, he was arrested!

Mike claimed the Turks shrugged at his American citizenship papers and were preparing to take him to jail when one of the police noticed his Marine Corps tie clasp and questioned him about it. Pointing to the tie clasp, he said, "You bet ya. I was a U.S. Marine!"

When repeating this story, his chest swelled as he uttered, "They let me go!"

Yuko

The Park Tavern's clientele was a mixed lot, and often changed with the time of day. The mid-morning and early afternoon crowd was mostly old-timers; many were foreign born, from Ireland or Eastern Europe. All were widowers or bachelors.

Some people called them the Sunshine Brigade. In the morning they would congregate on the west side of Main Street so they could soak up the sun. During the day they would gradually shift to the east side of the street, following the sun. If the day were cold or too hot, they would gradually find shelter in the Park Tavern. A few would have a draft beer; most would not.

Mike's draft beer was probably the worst in Park City. He used carbon dioxide as a propellant, the same as most saloons, but in between sales he would often turn off the gas. When he reopened the valve, there would be foam enough to fill a garbage can before a stream of foamy beer appeared. Mike would use a comb to rake the foam off the glass he was filling. It was a unique, somewhat disturbing, sight.

Some who gathered would bring their home-country newspapers, printed in their native tongues. Others would read the daily *Salt Lake Tribune* or the weekly *Park Record*. Once I sat next to Yuko Pezely. He was studying Safianides' Greek weekly newspaper. I asked, "Anything new happening?"

Yuko shrugged. "I don't know. It's all Greek to me!"

Yuko was Croatian and you could see him chuckling at his joke. He went back to studying the Greek newspaper, hoping someone else would ask him the same question.

Yuko was Si Pezely's brother. Si owned the New Deal Market at 204 Main Street; he borrowed the name from President Franklin Roosevelt's "New Deal" slogan.

Si was loud and political. He once ran for mayor on his New Deal Political Party ticket. He did not think the Democrats in power were really true Democrats.

Yuko was the complete opposite; he was quiet, reserved and soft-spoken and enjoyed a drink in the company of friends.

Justo

Justo Uriarte was cut somewhat from the same cloth as Yuko, with a keen sense of humor. He was a Basque native, a widower, and extremely proud of his family. Short, almost square in build, his drooping frame suggested that he was once a powerful man.

Justo was proud of his nationality. Once, Bob Mawhinney, who at the time was working as an aide at Holy Cross Hospital in Salt Lake City, lined up about five of us with dates from the hospital nursing school. Justo learned that one was a Basque national and thought she was my date. He lectured me on the fine quality of Basque women and urged me to court the Basque student nurse. I didn't have the heart to tell him my date was not the Basque.

A few years later Justo offered to sell me the Imperial Hotel, 221 Main Street, for $12,000. Oh how I wish I had taken him up on that offer. I'm sure the property is worth between five and eight million dollars in today's market. If my foresight ever catches up with my hindsight, I'll be wealthy.

Joe

Joe Dowd, another widower, was always well dressed. His thick glasses set him apart from many of his peers – that and the fact that he was a non-drinking Irishman. I guess he just enjoyed the atmosphere of a saloon and the company it provided. But, in all honesty, he was so quiet he seemed to blend into the woodwork.

Joe was always ready to lend a helping hand – even when he couldn't – such as the year that John Mitchell passed away. John's widow Winnie (Winifred) did not drive, but she kept their automobile in good running order and parked in front of her home at the top of Main Street so that, on occasion, some of her friends could take her for a drive and perhaps a stop at Lower Pop Jenks Café for coffee and a sandwich.

That worked great during the summer months, but with winter fast approaching she decided to put the car into storage. Winnie called Eley's Garage and asked if someone could pick up her car. Eley sent his son Fred, who was then a Summit County deputy sheriff but on occasional days off would help out his father.

Unfortunately, Fred drove his own car instead of the tow truck. On arriving, he realized his mistake.

Now, if there were anything happening in the neighborhood, Joe Dowd would be checking to see if he could be of any help. Fred asked Joe if he would drive Winnie's car down to the garage. Joe, being obliging, said he'd be glad to.

Back in the mid-1960s the turn-around at the top of Main Street was quite a bit different than it is today. It was somewhat narrower and, on the north (downhill) side, the road was braced up by a beautiful quarry-stone retaining wall that at the time was about six feet high.

Joe didn't hesitate. He slid into the driver's seat, pulled right out and, going a respectable 15 mph, made what you might call a beautiful swan dive right off the wall.

Winnie was afraid Joe might be injured and kept muttering, "The poor dear. The poor dear. He's always been a frail man. I'll be sure to pray for him." Then she asked Fred to phone the police.

Fred tried to explain that he was a deputy sheriff. He probably didn't want any of this to get back to Sheriff Ron Robinson, who was a stickler for law-and-order and keeping the ticket quota high.

And Joe, well, he just sat there in the driver's seat, grinning ear to ear, somewhat akin to the Cheshire cat in Alice in Wonderland. He seemed quite pleased with himself.

Deputy Fred walked down to the wreckage and asked, "What in the hell is wrong with you? Why did you drive off the embankment?"

Joe smiled a reply: "I thought I did pretty good for the first time I ever drove a car."

"Why in hell didn't you tell me you didn't know how to drive?"

"Don't know. Why didn't you ask me if I knew how to drive? But I think I'm getting the knack of it. I'll do better next time."

Fred hooked up the tow chain and told Joe that he would have to get out of the car. Joe frowned his disappointment. He dearly wanted to be towed down Main Street behind the steering wheel of the once-beautiful sedan.

Don't get me wrong. Befitting his Irish heritage, Joe liked a little mischief. For years he plagued Earl's Market (350 Main Street). When no one was watching, he would wind up the dozen or so alarm clocks on display and set the alarms to go off when Earl would be swamped with customers. Earl was at his wit's end. It took months before he suspected Joe and years to catch him in the act.

If you ever heard the expression "one-man parade," you might be surprised that many in Park City believed it was named for Joe. On his ninety-first birthday, which by chance fell on St. Patrick's Day, he staged a one-man parade down Main Street. Using his cane as a baton, he marched down the center line in rhythm with the honking horns of the swarming cars. Some say it was the best parade ever staged in the Park.

When Joe was in his mid-nineties he moved to Seattle to live with a daughter. He lived to be 107 years of age.

Pete

Pete Cunningham, a native of Cork, Ireland, was a regular at the Park Tavern. He was always dressed in a double-breasted dark suit, but often without a tie. His constant companion was a small black dog.

One day the dog was missing. Pete took the time to tell anyone listening that the dog was mad at him. "It happens every time I have a wee bit too much to drink," he explained. "Aye, that dog is worse than a wife; she will ignore me for two or three days 'til she gets over it. An' by then I'll go out again."

Actually, it wasn't Pete's dog. The dog belonged to Pete's landlord, Howard Anderson, who owned the Anderson Apartments across from the Post Office. But Howard's job took him out of town regularly and the dog thought Pete was good company.

I'm not sure what Pete did during his working career, but I do know that early on he was quite successful with the Salt Lake

Stock Exchange, which specialized in trading local mining stocks. But when the mineral market collapsed, I'm sure he was stuck with a lot of stock. I know from time to time he'd sell a few thousand shares for a fraction of what he had paid for them. The buyers usually were still-employed miners who thought the "camp" would boom in the future.

When Pete was a "wee bit under the influence," he was fun. The stories he told would hold the whole bar's attention, and with the punch line, the place would erupt in laughter. For the life of me, I can't remember any of his stories.

Pete had one song he would sing, if the right people asked him and if the mood struck him right. That song, I'm sure, was titled "Grandfather's Clock." And it took ten or more minutes of ... I guess it was mental preparation ... before he could perform.

He'd walk back and forth parallel to the bar – getting in synchronized rhythm with the ticking of a clock, a clock that was in his mind. He'd begin, "Hickory Dickery Dock, the mouse ran up the clock ..."

Everyone sitting at the bar would roar with laughter. It was funny, but to this day I'm not sure why. Maybe it was his deep Irish brogue. And maybe it was because Pete took it very seriously. Through it all he never cracked a smile. His singing was serious stuff, and yet he didn't seem to mind that others found it funny.

Afternoon Shift

As the afternoon advanced, a different type of clientele would begin drifting in. They were generally known as "winos" – hard drinkers who were on hard times. Most were lone men abandoned by family and friends who had formed a loose alliance with one another for mutual benefit, that benefit being booze.

Slim

There was John Wheeler, who answered to the name Slim. He lived at the Nelsons' ranch (now the base of the Park City Mountain resort). When sober, he worked as a handyman, first at the Nelsons' ranch. Later he worked a variety of jobs for John E. Fritch, who operated a service station and Dodge/Plymouth dealership below town.

Fritch also had a mine he was trying to develop in western Utah. It was close to the old ghost town of Gold Hill; other than that, it was in the middle of nowhere. At times Fritch would take, to his mine, a few old timers and winos who claimed they wanted a change of scenery and a chance to sober up. They would stay there for several weeks and looked great when they returned, but fell back into their old habits shortly thereafter.

During this time, I worked for Fritch as a service-station attendant while in high school and got acquainted with Slim and a few of his chums. When sober, Slim was hard working and a skilled craftsman. He could do near everything, and had the ability to figure the easiest way to do a job.

Fritch never tired of telling how Slim figured a shortcut method to pump the mine dry, which saved him both time and money. The lower portion of the mine was flooded. The water level stayed 50 feet from the bottom of the shaft. Each morning they would spend an hour or so pumping the water to the top of the shaft, a height of about 600 feet.

Slim suggested that they dam up the entrance to an abandoned drift (tunnel) that was only a few feet above the water level and pump the water there. Then, at quitting time, they would open the tunnel and let the water fill up the shaft.

Slim was the complete opposite when drinking. I remember one time when he waltzed into the Park Tavern with a large paper bag. You could hear the clinking of bottles as he passed by.

Larry Bye, a town roustabout, perked up and asked, "What you got there?"

"School books," replied a grinning Slim, "and I'm going to complete your education right now." They all but skipped as they left the Tavern. Mike frowned on all drinks that he did not pour and was getting ready to kick them out.

Once, late at night, following a heavy snow, I left the Park Tavern a few minutes after Slim. The newly-fallen snow was at least a foot deep and I tried to walk in Slim's footsteps. Now Slim stood about 6 foot 5 inches and was as thin as his name implied. And at that time of night his swagger turned into a stagger. Some of his footprints, I swear, were 6 feet apart and at times shot to the left or right at a 90-degree angle. I guess I should be happy I couldn't follow in Slim's footsteps.

Larry

Larry Bye was by far the most popular character who represented this unfortunate class of Park City's citizens. He may have been born with what is now called fetal alcohol syndrome. It was said he had a grandfather who wrote textbooks for the state of Indiana.

Larry always was outgoing and happy. He would work at any task you gave him, even if he had no idea what he was doing. He was in the CCC (Civilian Conservation Corps) during the Depression.

Somehow, Larry became the owner of a motorcycle, and he sometimes used it to harvest lumber. When the CCC cut ski runs in an area that was destined to become known as Snow Park, Larry attached a chain to logs and dragged them to the Tri-State Lumber yard at the intersection of Heber Avenue and Main Street. He claimed it was the best job he ever had and never tired of talking about it.

Larry served in the Army Air Corps during World War II. He also served as a volunteer fireman in the Park City Fire Department for years. And several times he was in the color guard during the July 4th or Labor Day parades.

I also found in a Silver King Coalition Mines Company "time book" that Larry had worked there as a mucker in February 1952. But I don't remember Larry talking about mining; I don't think he liked it.

In 1957, both Larry and Slim had bit parts in "Rusty and the Falcon," the first commercial movie ever shot in Park City, for Disney's "Wonderful World of Color." Their barroom acting was natural and stole the show.

Larry was one of the last bachelors to live on Easy Street, a rutted dirt road on the bank of Poison Creek. Most of the shacks had outhouses built over the creek. This old section parallels the new extension of lower Main Street. Much is now covered by Deer Valley Drive.

Park City was rapidly changing into a ski resort of some renown and, to some, the likes of Larry was an embarrassment. Some do-gooders decided Larry was a hazard to himself and the community at large and packed him off to a rest home in Heber. I got to visit Larry a few times after that. He seemed happy enough and told me they allowed him two cans of beer a day. I'm happy the state could afford that extravagance.

The Lunch-Bucket Brigade

At around five in the afternoon the Tavern would get a few miners coming off shift who some wag labeled the "lunch-bucket brigade." They were in no hurry to get home; some loved to mull over the events of the day, going over every detail of their shift. It was said that if they worked underground half as hard as the shift they put in at the saloons, they would be so tuckered out they wouldn't be hanging out in saloons. A few just didn't want to go home to howling kids and naggings wives. And some just wanted to relax over a cold beer and good conversation.

Among the steady customers were Mike and Johnny Byer, brothers in their mid-forties, hard-working miners who dreamed of striking it rich in their prospecting sideline.

Lynn & Alice

Around six o'clock Lynn Gordon would come in. Lynn was on crutches, suffering from some sort of debilitating arthritis. It would take him a little time to get set up at his blackjack table. He had to arrange his deck of cards just so, for easy access, and place his bottle of wine on the floor, out of sight but easy to reach. This done, he would place a Chesterfield cigarette in his ivory cigarette holder, sip his wine and look around for an easy mark.

A short time later, Lynn's estranged wife, Alice, would show up. Alice was a huge woman who moved in a slow, heavy manner. She handled the crap table when it was uncovered.

The city imposed an automatic 25-dollar fine when the cover was removed. Mike had to have a full house and people clamoring to play before the cover was taken off. Then Alice came alive, donning a bright green visor cap, cane in hand, and unleashing a whole repertoire of words pertaining to the art of dice throwing.

In hindsight, I came to appreciate her chatter. I watched and studied the game for hours, but played it only once. Damn, it's sobering to see how fast money can vanish!

During those busy nights, Mike often employed a barmaid to help out. The two I remember were Alice Brennan and Sara Thompson. Both were fun-loving divorcees who felt lucky to find part-time employment doing anything in the old "camp".

I held Sara in awe after I heard she had run off some would-be thugs by taking an unopened can of beer and squashing it until it burst as she told them to get out! Now, back in the '50s, all beverage cans were made of steel, not the thin-wall aluminum of today. Whether it was an old can or some sort of trick, I cannot say. But the thugs climbed over one another beating an exit. I always conducted myself as a gentleman when Sara was behind the bar.

A few years later Sara married Ray Beckstead, the father of my good friend Raymond.

Eddy

Eddy Hawkinson, a bachelor who worked at the Silver King Mine, had few wants and spent his money frugally. The trouble was he'd forget to cash his paychecks and they would accumulate in a haphazard manner in a dresser drawer. When he cashed one, it was often the current check, leaving some checks a year old or more. It became a bookkeeper's nightmare at the mine and they threatened to fire Eddy if he didn't cash his checks. He complied, but never forgave the mining company.

Eddy did not trust banks and thought 3½ percent interest paid on a passbook saving account was a joke. But he didn't want to hide the money in his mattress, so he went ahead and opened a savings account in the local bank.

Eddy would stop in the Tavern and order a shot or two of whiskey with a Coca-Cola chaser. That is if Mike had bottled Coke. Eddy collected Coke bottles from around the world. He had bottles from forty-eight states and a couple of territories, plus several foreign countries. He never tired of talking about his collection. He kept them stored on the back porch of his house.

I often wondered what happened to his collection after his death. I imagined the distant relative who inherited his estate not knowing their uniqueness and taking them to the local market for the deposit refund.

Eddy claimed that one of his first jobs as a young man was helping to transport the ball mill piece-by-piece to the Silver King Mine. Since he knew my grandfather owned a livery stable and did much of his hauling by horse, Eddy presumed that the art of being a teamster must be one of my great interests. Hell, my knowledge of horses was negligible, and that of wagons and freight was nonexistent.

Eddy would always ignore the glazed expression on my face as he took a pinch of Copenhagen snuff, placed it below his tongue, and launched into his well-rehearsed lecture on the art of teamstering. He spoke of the many tons of this load and the hundred or so horses it took to pull the load. Not ordinary horses, but Morgans and Clydesdales. He spoke of the clothing the teamsters wore, especially the six-to-eight-inch-wide belt that marked, with pride, their profession.

I asked, "Why such a wide belt?"

Eddy shot back, "To hold their guts in! The shaking and bouncing on big rigs without springs was horrid!"

He would tell me how the wagons were rigged, and the names of various parts: sizes, axels, wheels, and things called trees. I'd smile and nod and pretend to be listening. But, in truth, it was lost on me.

In hindsight, I was an idiot. A few years back, I wrote an article about stagecoaches and discovered I knew nothing about them. The language, terminology and methods used in their construction left me with more questions than answers. I wished Eddy had lived long enough to help me out.

Rusty

Rusty Prudence would stop by Mike's on occasion. He spent time in every saloon in town. Rusty liked people and enjoyed visiting. He greeted everyone with, "Hello neighbor!" and often picked up the conversation where it had ended six months earlier. If his sister Alice was tending bar, Rusty would be there. I think Alice would slip Rusty free beers when Mike was not looking.

Rusty carried the nickname "Rags" because his clothes were often tattered. In the heat of summer he often would go without a shirt. I'm not sure if Rusty thought he looked good going shirtless or was indifferent to his looks, but I know he took pride in his hairy chest.

One hot evening, after the televised fights were over, our conversation began to sag. I thought I would do something I saw in the Navy. I had a shipmate who often would take his cigarette lighter and light one of his hairy legs afire. It always would flare up, then go out on its own.

Unfortunately, or fortunately, I did not have enough hair to practice on myself. I reached over and set Rusty's chest ablaze. If I remember right, it took the better part of a glass of beer to put Rusty out!

Other than losing a chestful of hair and suddenly feeling naked, Rusty was all right. But I felt bad. I apologized and apologized.

It didn't do much good. Rusty went from surprise to shock to anger. He demanded to know why I would do such a stupid thing. I tried to explain about my friend in the Navy. Rusty cut me short by declaring that he had spent more time in the Navy than I had and he had never seen any such foolery.

I was at a loss for words. All I could do was buy him beer after beer for the rest of the night. For the next six months or so, every time I bumped into Rags he would bring up the subject and I would end up buying him beer. If a lesson was learned, it was that I should never, ever play with fire.

Weekends

On weekends, a few married couples would stop by the Park Tavern for a few drinks and to dance. Mike had a great dance floor in the southeast corner of the building. There was a chandelier with ten or so colored lights that were wired to flicker in synchronized patterns. Ray's Music, a jukebox company, kept the latest popular records on the Tavern's jukebox. I remember Jim and Emma Christensen preferred western or country music. Other couples are now just shadows in my mind.

About the Author

The author as a high school senior in 1955.
Photo courtesy of the Kimball Archive.

Gary Austin Kimball loved Park City and he loved history. He merged these two passions when he wrote about Park City's colorful past, often focusing on the minorities who worked in the mines, stores and saloons. His stories were published in *Lodestar Magazine* (now *Park City Magazine*) and *The Park Record*. He was the author of several books including "Death and Dying in Old Park City" in 2005, "Of Moths and Miners" in 2006 and "Life under China Bridge" in 2013.

Gary took an interest in community issues and belonged to many social justice organizations. He served on the Park City

Historic District Commission. In August 2009 the Park City Council proclaimed him the town's historian or, as the mayor said, "Ye Official Old Guy."

A fourth-generation Park City native, Gary lived all his life in Park City except for time spent in college and in the Navy. His formative years began at the height of the Great Depression and spanned the 1940s and early 1950s.

Park City was a very different place then. Gary attended the Marsac School before it became City Hall and Park City High School before it became the library. He graduated from high school in 1955 with classmates whom he admired and loved.

Gary was a character who enjoyed a beverage and good conversation. He held many different jobs in Park City including lift operator, insurance salesman and Grubstake Grocery store co-owner. He also worked for Chevron Pipeline for 23 years.

Gary was born at home on April 30, 1937, to Maud and Gilbert Kimball. He grew up with a sister, Helen, and brothers Paul and Gilbert Jr. He was married to Jane Ann Jennings Kimball for 52 years. They had two children, James Patrick and Janice Jennings Kimball. He died on June 5, 2018.

Acknowledgements
James Kimball

David Hampshire, without you this project would not have seen the light of day. Thanks for your vision, attention to detail and coming up with the book's title. I would also like to thank:

Katie Mullaly, Surrogate Press
Harley Campos
Park City Museum
Summit County Museum
Dolly's Bookstore/Michaela
Park City Class of 1955
Jim Jennings
Bob Mawhinney
Mary Lou Toly
Paul Kimball
Kimball Family
Peters Family
Jane Meade
Kamen Goddard
Miller Heritage
Robert Stewart
Don Weller

James Kimball, 2022